W9-BLN-056

Active

Second Edition

LISTENING

3

STEVEN BROWN

DOROLYN SMITH

CAMBRIDGE
UNIVERSITY PRESS

University Printing House, Cambridge CB2 8BS, United Kingdom

One Liberty Plaza, 20th Floor, New York, NY 10006, USA

477 Williamstown Road, Port Melbourne, VIC 3207, Australia

4843/24, 2nd Floor, Ansari Road, Daryaganj, Delhi – 110002, India

79 Anson Road, #06–04/06, Singapore 079906

Cambridge University Press is part of the University of Cambridge.

It furthers the University's mission by disseminating knowledge in the pursuit of education, learning and research at the highest international levels of excellence.

www.cambridge.org
Information on this title: www.cambridge.org/9780521678216

© Cambridge University Press 2007

This publication is in copyright. Subject to statutory exception and to the provisions of relevant collective licensing agreements, no reproduction of any part may take place without the written permission of Cambridge University Press.

First published 2007
20 19 18 17 16 15

Printed in Great Britain by CPI Group (UK) Ltd, Croydon CR0 4YY

A catalogue record for this publication is available from the British Library

ISBN 978-0-521-67817-9 student's book and self-study audio CD
ISBN 978-0-521-67818-6 teacher's manual and audio CD
ISBN 978-0-521-67819-3 CDs (audio)

Cambridge University Press has no responsibility for the persistence or accuracy of URLs for external or third-party internet websites referred to in this publication, and does not guarantee that any content on such websites is, or will remain, accurate or appropriate.

Art direction and book design: Adventure House, NYC
Layout services: Page Designs International
Audio production: Full House, NYC
Illustrations: William Waitzman

Contents

Plan of the book

Unit	Listening tasks	Listening skills	Speaking	Pronunciation
Before you begin Getting ready to listen and learn pages 2–5	1 What do you need to know? 2 What do you already know?	Reasons for listening Thinking about what you already know Predicting		
1 What do you say first? pages 6–9	1 A good first impression 2 Keep the conversation going.	Details Inference Main idea Inference	**We have a lot in common.** Practicing conversation patterns with classmates	Intonation of questions
2 Sights and sounds pages 10–13	1 The five senses 2 The smell of money	Inference Details Main idea Details	**Sales sense** Designing a product that appeals to the senses	Vowel sounds
3 Dating pages 14–17	1 Which way is best? 2 How did they meet?	Main idea Inference Main idea Details	**My best match** Sharing information about what is important in a partner	Intonation of lists
4 Communication and culture pages 18–21	1 I just don't understand. 2 It's our style.	Main idea Details Main idea Details	**Good communication** Sharing tips for good communication	/t/ in *shouldn't*
Expansion 1 Russia pages 22–23	Information and an authentic student interview about dating and marriage traditions			
5 The Internet pages 24–27	1 Great site! 2 The growth of the Internet	Inference Details	**My homepage** Designing a homepage	Linked sounds
6 Superstitions pages 28–31	1 Around the world 2 The real meaning	Main idea Inference Main idea Details	**Are you superstitious?** Playing a board game	Regular rhythm of stressed words
7 Manners pages 32–35	1 It drives me crazy! 2 Mind your manners.	Main idea Inference Main idea Details	**It really bothers me.** Sharing situations that drive you crazy	Emphasis to express strong emotion
8 Natural health pages 36–39	1 Reflexology 2 Staying healthy	Main idea Details Inference Details	**A day at my spa** Designing a spa schedule	Intonation of thought groups
Expansion 2 Ireland pages 40–41	Information and an authentic student interview about superstitions			

Acknowledgments

Text credits

47 Green Giant® is a registered trademark of General Mills and is used with permission.

47 ExxonMobil is used with permission.

47 Sara Lee is used with permission.

47 VISA is used with permission.

70 Starbucks® is a registered trademark of Starbucks Corporation and is used with permission.

Illustration credits

Kenneth Batelman: 55, 56
CB Canga: 30
James Elston: 7, 61
Chuck Gonzales: 3, 72, 73

Ben Kirchner: 18, 19, 33
Frank Montagna: 10, 11, 24, 31, 34, 57, 67
Terry Wong: 65
Filip Yip: 28, 29, 62

Photography credits

5 (*top to bottom*) © Corbis; © Punchstock
6 © John Giustina/Getty Images
8 © John Giustina/Getty Images
10 (*clockwise from top left*) © Corbis; © Marie-Louise Avery/Alamy; © Age fotostock; © Punchstock; © Jupiter Images; © Photos.com; © Punchstock; © Carl Purcell/Corbis; © Punchstock; © Istock
11 © Digital Vision
12 © Reuters/Corbis
14 © Spencer Rowell/Getty Images
15 (*clockwise from left*) © Steve Niedorf/Getty Images; © Jupiter Images; © Getty Images
16 (*left to right*) © Index Stock; © Jupiter Images
20 (*left to right*) © Livia Corona/Getty Images; © Photos.com; © Upper Cut/© Punchstock
22 © Corbis
23 (*both*) © Peter Turnley/Corbis
25 © Punchstock
26 (*left to right*) © Age fotostock; © Punchstock
32 © Jupiter Images
34 © Jupiter Images
36 (*clockwise from top right*) © Age fotostock; © Corbis; © Pierre Bourrier/Getty Images; © Jupiter Images; © Punchstock; © Punchstock; © Alamy; © Age fotostock; © Alamy
38 (*left, top to bottom*) © Spencer Jones/Getty Images; © Corbis; (*middle*) © Richard Leo Johnson/Getty Images; (*right, top to bottom*) © Marc Romanelli/Getty Images; © Age fotostock
40 © Paul Harris/Getty Images
41 (*clockwise from left*) © Paul Hart/Alamy; © Oliver Benn/Getty Images; © Mango Productions/Corbis; © Jon Shireman/Getty Images

42 (*top to bottom*) © Will Crocker/Getty Images; © Istock; © Photospin
43 (*clockwise from top left*) © Age fotostock; © Jim Zuckerman/Corbis; © Age fotostock; © Michael Abbinante/Alamy; © Punchstock; © Age fotostock
44 © Tom Walker/Getty Images
46 (*clockwise from top left*) © Reuters/Corbis; © Dana O'Malley; © Istock; © Age fotostock; © Jupiter Images; © Getty Images
48 © AP Wide World Photos
50 © Danielle Power
51 (*top to bottom*) © Peter Cook/Alamy; © Jupiter Images
52 © Masterfile
54 (*left to right*) © Newscom; © Newscom; © Alamy
58 (*left to right*) © National Geographic Society; © David A. Northcott/Corbis
59 © Jupiter Images
64 (*clockwise from left*) © Alamy; © Masterfile; © Jupiter Images; © Jim Craigmyle/Corbis
66 (*top*) © Punchstock; (*bottom, both*) © Jupiter Images
68 © Jupiter Images
69 © Corbis
70 © Punchstock
74 (*clockwise from left*) © Jason Hawkes/Corbis; © Photo Researchers; © Photospheres
76 (*left to right*) © Jupiter Images; © Michelle Falzone/Alamy
77 © Alamy

Author acknowledgments

We would like to thank our **reviewers** for their helpful suggestions:
Andrew Newton, **Sogang University**, Seoul, South Korea
Yao-feng Huang, **Tajen University**, Pingtung, Taiwan
Gordon Sites, **Keihoku Junior High School**, Chiba, Japan
Brooks Slaybaugh, **Tamagawa Gakuen**, Tokyo, Japan
David Philip, **Pusan National University**, Pusan, South Korea
Robert Bendergrass, **Pukyong National University**, Pusan, South Korea

We would also like to acknowledge the **students** and **teachers** in the following schools and institutes who piloted components of the first edition of *Active Listening*:

Alianza Cultural Uruguay-Estados Unidos, Montevideo, Uruguay; **Bae Centre**, Buenos Aires, Argentina; **Bunka Institute of Foreign Languages**, Tokyo, Japan; **Educational Options**, Santa Clara, California, U.S.A.; **Impact English**, Santiago, Chile; **Instituto Cultural de Idiomas Ltda.**, Caxias do Sul, Brazil; **Kansai University of Foreign Studies**, Osaka, Japan; **Koyo Choji Co. Ltd.**, Hitachi, Japan; **National Chin-Yi Institute of Technology**, Taichung, Taiwan; **Osaka Institute of Technology**, Osaka, Japan; **Southern Illinois University**, Niigata, Japan; **Suzugamine Women's College**, Hiroshima City, Japan; **Tokyo Foreign Language College**, Tokyo, Japan; **Umeda Business College**, Osaka, Japan; **University of Michigan English Language Institute**, Ann Arbor, Michigan, U.S.A.

Thanks also go to those **interviewed** for the **Expansion** units: Morris Senkichi Kimura, Lyudmila Kytasty, Neil O'Flaherty, Jackeline Silva, and to the English Language Institute at the University of Pittsburgh for support during this project.

A special thanks to the **editorial** and **production** team at Cambridge University Press who worked on this edition:
Eleanor Barnes, David Bohlke, Karen Brock, Rob Freire, Deborah Goldblatt, Yuri Hara, Louisa Hellegers, Lise Minovitz, Sandra Pike, Danielle Power, Tami Savir, Jaimie Scanlon, Kayo Taguchi, Louisa van Houten, and Dorothy Zemach. This book is much better because of their careful work and helpful insights.

Thanks to the Cambridge University Press **staff** and **advisors**:
Harry Ahn, Yumiko Akeba, Michelle Kim, Andy Martin, Nigel McQuitty, Carine Mitchell, Mark O'Neil, Rebecca Ou, Bruno Paul, Dan Schulte, Catherine Shih, Howard Siegelman, and Ivan Sorrentino.

Very special thanks to Deborah Goldblatt, who has been enthusiastic about this project for longer than she would have preferred. Thanks for her patience and her support over the years.

Finally, we would like to acknowledge and thank Marc Helgesen for his role as author on the first edition. He's remained a great friend and source of ideas throughout the writing of this book.

To the teacher

Active Listening, Second Edition is a fully updated and revised edition of the popular three-level listening series for adult and young adult learners of North American English. Each level offers students 16 engaging, task-based units, each built around a topic, function, or grammatical theme. Grounded in the theory that learners are more successful listeners when they activate their prior knowledge of a topic, the series gives students a frame of reference to make predictions about what they will hear. Through a careful balance of activities, students learn to listen for main ideas, to listen for details, and to listen and make inferences.

Active Listening, Second Edition Level 3 is intended for intermediate to high-intermediate students. It can be used as a main text for listening classes or as a component in speaking or integrated-skills classes.

The second edition differs from the first in a number of ways. In recent years, there has been a greater emphasis on the role of vocabulary and pronunciation in the field of second language acquisition. To reflect this emphasis, the second edition provides a more refined vocabulary syllabus and a more extensive preview of words. The final section of each unit has also been expanded to provide a full-page speaking activity, including pronunciation practice. In addition, the Listening tasks in each unit have been expanded. Students listen to the same input twice, each time listening for a different purpose and focusing on a listening skill appropriate for that purpose. Other changes in the second edition include the systematic integration of cultural information. Most units contain interesting cultural information in the listening tasks, and a new, two-page Expansion unit containing cultural information about a country or region of the world and an authentic student interview, has been added after every four units to review and extend the language and topics of the previous units. Each unit also has a Self-study page, accompanied by an audio CD, that can be used for self-study or homework.

ABOUT THE BOOK

The book includes 16 core units and four expansion units. Each core unit has four parts: **Warming up,** two main **Listening tasks,** and **Your turn to talk,** a speaking activity for pairs or small groups. The four **Expansion** units present cultural information related to the unit themes. In addition, there is an introductory lesson called **Before you begin.** This lesson introduces students to helpful learning strategies and types of listening.

The units can be taught in the order presented or out of sequence to follow the themes of the class or another book it is supplementing. In general, the tasks in the second half of the book are more challenging than those in the first, and language from earlier units is recycled as the book progresses.

Unit organization

Each unit begins with an activity called **Warming up.** This activity, usually done in pairs, serves two purposes: It reminds students of what they already know about the topic, and it previews common vocabulary used in the unit. When they do the warming up activity, students use their prior knowledge, or "schema," about the topic, vocabulary, and structures, as well as learn new vocabulary and phrases that are connected to the theme of the unit. The combination of the two approaches makes the listening tasks that follow easier.

Listening task 1 and **Listening task 2** are the major listening exercises. Each task has two parts. The students work with the same input in both parts of the task, but they listen for different reasons each time. The tasks are balanced to include a variety of listening skills, which are identified in a box to the left of each listening exercise. Because *Active Listening* features a task-based approach, students should do the activities as they listen, rather than wait until they have finished listening to a particular segment.

Your turn to talk, the final section of each unit, is a short, fluency-oriented speaking task done in pairs or small groups. First, students *prepare* for the speaking activity by gathering ideas and thinking about the topic. Next, they *practice* a pronunciation point. Finally, they *speak* to their classmates as they exchange information or opinions.

The two-page **Expansion** unit after every four units features listening activities that provide general cultural information about a country or region of the world and an authentic interview with a person from that place. The tasks focus on the same listening skills as the core units and recycle the themes and topics of the preceding four units.

The **Self-study** page reviews language, vocabulary, and themes from the unit and provides personalization exercises. It can be used for homework or for additional listening practice in class.

Hints and techniques

■ Be sure to do the **Warming up** section for each unit. This preview can help students develop useful learning strategies. It also helps students to be more successful listeners, which, in turn, motivates and encourages them.

■ Try to play a particular segment only one or two times. If students are still having difficulty, try telling them the answers. Then play the audio again and let them experience understanding what they heard previously.

■ If some students find listening very difficult, have them do the task in pairs, helping each other as necessary. The **Teacher's Manual,** described in the box in the next column, contains additional ideas.

■ Some students may not be used to active learning. Those students may be confused by your instructions, since they are used to a more passive role. Explaining activities verbally is usually the least effective way to give instructions. It is better to demonstrate. For example, read the instructions as briefly as possible (e.g., "Listen. Number the

pictures."). Then play the first part of the audio program. Stop the recording and elicit the correct answer from the students. Those who weren't sure what to do will quickly understand. The same techniques work for **Warming up** and **Your turn to talk.** Lead one pair or group through the first step of the task. As the other students watch, they will quickly see what they are supposed to do.

Active Listening, Second Edition Level 3 is accompanied by a Teacher's Manual that contains step-by-step teaching notes with key words highlighted, optional speaking activities and listening strategies, photocopiable unit quizzes for each Student's Book unit, and two complete photocopiable tests with audio CD.

HOW STUDENTS LEARN TO LISTEN

Many students find listening to be one of the most difficult skills in English. The following explains some of the ideas incorporated into the book to make students become more effective listeners. *Active Listening, Second Edition* Level 3 is designed to help students make real and rapid progress. Recent research into teaching listening and its related receptive skill, reading, has given insights into how successful students learn foreign or second languages.

Bottom-up vs. top-down processing: a brick-wall analogy

To understand what our students are going through as they learn to listen or read, consider the "bottom-up vs. top-down processing" distinction. The distinction is based on the ways students process and attempt to understand what they read or hear. With bottom-up processing, students start with the component parts: words, grammar, and the like. Top-down processing is the opposite. Students start from their background knowledge.

This might be better understood by means of a metaphor. Imagine a brick wall. If you are standing at the bottom looking at the wall brick by brick, you can easily see the details. It is difficult, however, to get an overall view of the wall. And, if you come to a missing brick (e.g., an unknown word or unfamiliar structure), you're stuck. If, on the other hand, you're sitting on the top of the wall, you can easily see the landscape. Of course, because of distance, you'll miss some details.

Students, particularly those with years of "classroom English" but little experience in really using the language, try to listen from the "bottom up."

They attempt to piece the meaning together, word by word. It is difficult for us, as native and advanced non-native English users, to experience what students go through. However, try reading the following *from right to left.*

> word one ,slowly English process you When
> to easy is it ,now doing are you as ,time a at
> .word individual each of meaning the catch
> understand to difficult very is it ,However
> .passage the of meaning overall the

You were probably able to understand the paragraph:

> When you process English slowly, one word
> at a time, as you are doing now, it is easy to
> catch the meaning of each individual word.
> However, it is very difficult to understand
> the overall meaning of the passage.

While reading, however, it is likely you felt the frustration of bottom-up processing; you had to get each individual part before you could make sense of it. This is similar to what our students experience – and they're having to wrestle the meaning in a foreign language. Of course, this is an ineffective way to listen since it takes too long. While students are still trying to make sense of what has been said, the speaker keeps going. The students get lost.

Although their processing strategy makes listening difficult, students do come to class with certain strengths. From their years of English study, most have a relatively large, if passive, vocabulary. They also often have a solid receptive knowledge of English grammar. We shouldn't neglect the years of life experience; our students bring with them a wealth of background knowledge on many topics. These three strengths – vocabulary, grammar, and life experience – can be the tools for effective listening.

The **Warming up** activities in *Active Listening* build on those strengths. By engaging the students in active, meaningful prelistening tasks, students integrate bottom-up and top-down processing. They start from meaning, but, in the process of doing the task, use vocabulary and structures (grammar) connected with the task, topic, or function. The result is an integrated listening strategy.

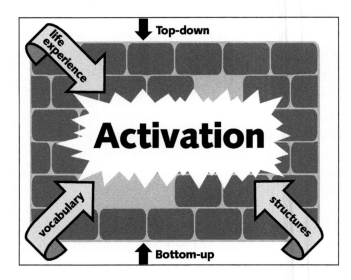

Types of listening

A second factor that is essential in creating effective listeners is exposing them to a variety of types of listening. Many students have only had experience with listening for literal comprehension. While listening for details, or specific information, is an important skill, it represents only one type. We have attempted to reach a balance in the book in order to give students experience with – and an understanding of – listening for the main idea, or gist, and listening and making inferences. Students usually are quick to understand the idea of listening for the main idea. They can easily imagine having to catch the general meaning of something they hear. Inference – listening "between the lines" – can be more difficult. We need to remember listening is actually very complex.

Remember that although listeners need practice in listening, they also need more: They need to learn *how* to listen. They need different types of listening strategies and tasks. They need to learn to preview. Our students need exposure to it all. When students get the exposure they need, they build their listening skills. They become active listeners.

Listening training tips

These are techniques you can use with your students so they become better listeners.

Listen in pairs. People usually think of listening as a solo skill – students do it alone even if they are in a room with lots of other learners. If a listening is challenging, try having students do the task in pairs. Each pair uses only one book. That way, learners help each other by pointing out what they understood rather than worrying about what they missed.

Do something physical. If a particular listening segment is very difficult, pick a specific item (colors, place names, dates, etc.) that occurs four to eight times. Have students close their books. Then play the audio program. Have students do a physical action, such as tapping their desks or raising their hand each time they hear the target item. The task is focused enough that most learners can accomplish it. The physical action gives immediate feedback and support to learners who missed it on the audio program.

Choose an appropriate level of support. After students have heard a segment, check it as a group. Write the answers on the board. Then play the audio program again. Learners choose their own level of support. Those who basically understood close their eyes and imagine the conversations. Those who understood some look at their books and try to hear the items mentioned. Those who found it quite challenging should watch you. As you play the audio program, point to the information on the board just before it is mentioned.

Listen a month later. If your students found a particular segment very challenging, go back after a month or two and play it again. They will usually find it much easier than when they heard it the first time. It helps students see their own progress.

Do not look at the audioscript. Generally, don't give students the audioscript. It reinforces word and sentence-level (bottom-up) processing and reinforces the myth that learners can't understand meaning without catching everything they hear.

Steven Brown
Dorolyn Smith

Before you begin

Getting ready to listen and learn

From the people who wrote this book

Dear Students:

You've learned a lot of English so far. We hope this book will help you learn even more. We also hope that you enjoy learning it.

Before you begin, we would like to give you some hints about learning how to listen. First of all, it is important to think about your task. <u>Why</u> are you listening? What do you need to know?

Work with a partner.

You want to take an English class. What do you need to know? Write the questions you need to ask.

<u>What time are the classes?</u>

_____

_____

_____

What is the most important question for you? Check (✓) it.

You also need to think about your knowledge. What do you already know? To help you answer this question, each of the units in this book begins with a Warming up activity. This helps you think about the words and ideas you will hear. It makes listening and understanding easier.

We hope you will be <u>active</u> when you listen. Sometimes you will work in pairs or small groups. Help your partners. Listen to their ideas. When you don't understand something, ask your teacher or another student.

Good luck with learning English. You can do it!

Sincerely,

Steven Brown

Dorolyn Smith

What do you need to know?

We listen for different reasons.

A Work with a partner. Look at the ad. What questions might people ask about this apartment? Why? Write the questions and reasons.

APARTMENT FOR RENT
Call 555-2938

questions	reasons
How big is the apartment?	_The family has three children._
_____	_____
_____	_____

B 🎧 Listen. People are calling about the apartment. What's the most important question for each person? Why? Write the questions and reasons.

1. _Are pets OK_____?
   _She has a cat_____.

2. _____?
   _____
   _____.

3. _____?
   _____
   _____.

4. _____?
   _____
   _____.

5. _____?
   _____
   _____.

What do you already know?

Before you listen, you need to think about what you already know.

A Read the message below.

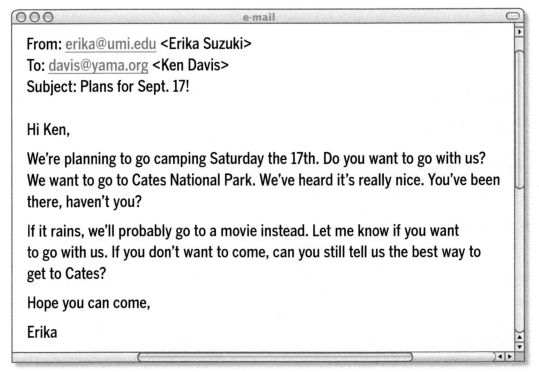

From: erika@umi.edu <Erika Suzuki>
To: davis@yama.org <Ken Davis>
Subject: Plans for Sept. 17!

Hi Ken,

We're planning to go camping Saturday the 17th. Do you want to go with us? We want to go to Cates National Park. We've heard it's really nice. You've been there, haven't you?

If it rains, we'll probably go to a movie instead. Let me know if you want to go with us. If you don't want to come, can you still tell us the best way to get to Cates?

Hope you can come,

Erika

B Look at the map and ticket. What do you think Ken will tell Erika?

ROUTE 5

CATES NATIONAL PARK

ROUTE 12

$30.00 SEC 214
17 SEPT 8:00 P.M.

IN CONCERT:
COSMOS
SATURDAY,
SEPTEMBER 17
8:00 P.M.
SUN HALL
124367565483

What do you already know?

C Erika is talking to Ken. Look at Erika's questions. If you know Ken's answers, check (✓) them.

1. "What are you doing today, Ken?"

   ☐ "I'm going to work soon."

   ☐ "I have class this afternoon."

2. "You've been to Cates National Park, right?"

   ☐ "Yes. I went last summer."

   ☐ "No. I've never been there before."

3. "What's the fastest way to get there?"

   ☐ "Take Route 12."

   ☐ "Take Route 5."

4. "Would you like to go with us on the 17th?"

   ☐ "I'd love to."

   ☐ "I'd really like to, but I can't."

5. "What are you doing that day?"

   ☐ "I have to work."

   ☐ "I'm going to a concert."

6. "How about the weekend after that?"

   ☐ "That sounds good."

   ☐ "Sorry. I'm busy then, too."

D 🎧 Now listen to their conversation. Check (✓) the answers you didn't know.

What do you say first?

A What do you do when you meet someone for the first time? Check (✓) the things you do. Then compare your answers with a partner.

- ☐ ask the other person questions
- ☐ comment about the weather
- ☐ introduce myself and say my name
- ☐ keep the conversation going as long as possible
- ☐ shake hands
- ☐ smile and make eye contact
- ☐ tell the person about myself
- ☐ try to find something in common with the person
- ☐ try to use the person's name in the conversation

B What topics do you like to talk about with someone you've just met? Write as many as you can.

my hometown

A good first impression

DETAILS **A** 🎧 Listen. People are talking about strategies they use to make a good first impression. Complete their examples.

1 Use people's names.

"Nice to meet you, _____*Rei*_____ ." **OR**
"So, _____*Rei*_____ , where do you work?"

2 Add extra information.

"Yes, I do. I like this music, but I really like _____ , too. That's my _____ ."

3 Find something in common.

"Have you ever taken a _____ with this _____ before?"

4 Ask about the other person.

"So, _____ are you _____?" **OR**
"What do you _____?" **OR**
"Are you a _____ _____?"

INFERENCE **B** 🎧 Now listen to four other conversations. Which strategies from Exercise A do the speakers use? Write the strategies.

1. *Find something in common.*

2. _____

3. _____

4. _____

Keep the conversation going.

MAIN IDEA **A** Listen. People are meeting for the first time. How do they keep the conversations going? Number the strategies in the correct order from 1 to 3.

1. _2_ say their names
   _1_ comment about the place
   _3_ talk about something they have in common

3. ____ add extra information
   ____ ask a question
   ____ say their names

2. ____ say their names
   ____ comment about the weather
   ____ ask a question

4. ____ comment about the place
   ____ say their names
   ____ talk about something they have in common

INFERENCE **B** Listen again. Do you think the conversations will continue? Check (✓) *yes* or *no*.

	yes	no		yes	no
1.	✓	☐	3.	☐	☐
2.	☐	☐	4.	☐	☐

SELF-STUDY *See page 84.*

We have a lot in common.

PREPARE **A** Work with a partner. Read the strategies and examples for starting a conversation. Then add one example for each strategy.

Comment about the weather or the place.	Introduce yourself and say your name.
• Nice day today, isn't it? • This is a great school, don't you think so? • _____	• Hi. I don't think we've met. I'm Lee. • _____
Try to find something in common.	**Ask about the other person.**
• I'm a soccer fan. How about you? • _____	• So, are you from around here? • _____

PRACTICE **B** **1.** 🎧 Listen and practice. Notice the intonation of questions.

How long have you studied English?   What's your favorite sport?

Do you have any sisters?   Have you ever done a homestay?

2. 🎧 Listen. Do you hear a question? Check (✓) *yes* or *no*.

	yes	no			yes	no			yes	no
a.	✓	☐		c.	☐	☐		e.	☐	☐
b.	☐	☐		d.	☐	☐		f.	☐	☐

SPEAK **C** Go around the class. Choose a conversation pattern below and start a conversation with a classmate. Then change partners and try a different conversation pattern.

Pattern 1	Pattern 2	Pattern 3
Comment about the weather.	Introduce yourself.	Comment about the place.
Ask about the other person.	Ask about the other person.	Introduce yourself.
Introduce yourself.	Find something in common.	Ask about the other person.

Nice day today, isn't it?

It sure is.

So, are you from around here?

Sights and sounds

A Think about your five senses: hearing, sight, smell, taste, and touch. Then add at least one more word for each sense.

The Five Senses

Hearing	Sight	Smell	Taste	Touch
loud	bright	strong	bitter	rough
quiet	dark	sweet	sour	soft
noisy				

B Work with a partner. Take turns choosing one of the pictures and describing it. Can your partner guess which picture it is?

This feels very soft. It's a pet and . . .

Is it a kitten?

This	⌐ sounds . . .
	looks . . .
	smells . . .
	tastes . . .
	⌐ feels . . .

The five senses

INFERENCE **A** 🎧 **Listen. Which sense is the speaker talking about? Number the senses from 1 to 4. Then write the words that gave you the hints. (There is one extra sense.)**

_____ hearing _____

_____ smell   _____

_____ sight   _____

_____ touch   _____

__1__ taste   _food, sugar, salt_____

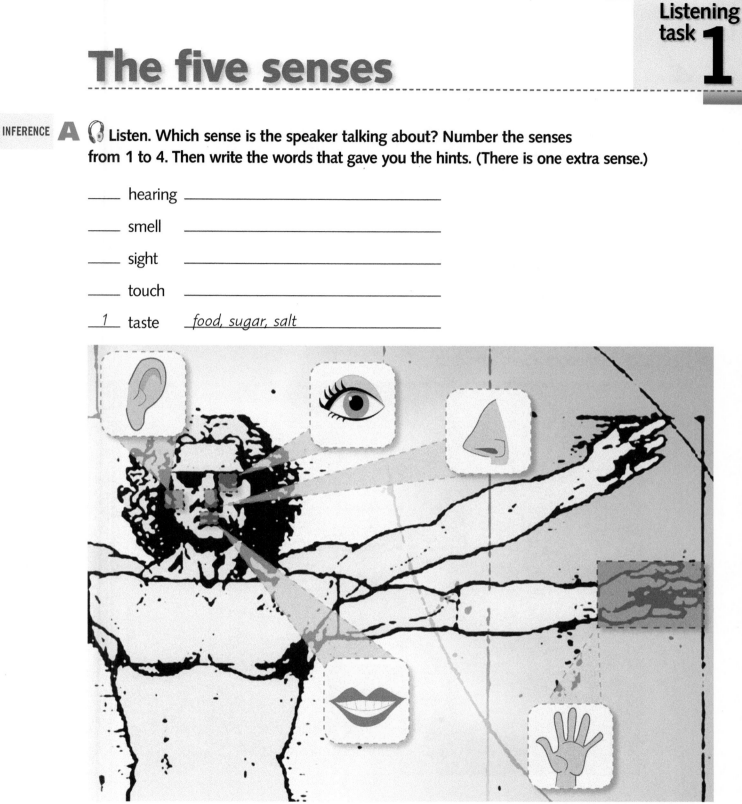

Source: Leonardo da Vinci's *Vitruvian Man*

DETAILS **B** 🎧 **Listen again. Are the statements true or false? Check (✓) the correct answers.**

	true	false
1. We often want to eat sweet foods after we exercise.	☐	☑
2. Babies use this sense to recognize their mothers.	☐	☐
3. This sense is stronger for humans than for dolphins.	☐	☐
4. Humans use this sense the most.	☐	☐

2 The smell of money

MAIN IDEA **A** 🎧 **Listen. How can the senses affect shoppers? Number the items from 1 to 4. (There is one extra item.)**

by influencing . . .

_____ the decision-making process

_____ ideas about the quality of a product

_____ beliefs about brands

_1_ beliefs about the value of a product

_____ emotions about a product

DETAILS **B** 🎧 **Listen again. Circle the correct information.**

1. The smell made people think the price was (higher)/ lower.

2. *Loud / Soft* music sometimes helps stores make money.

3. Some companies require employees to wear certain *hairstyles / uniforms*.

4. Some car companies create a special sound for the car *door / horn*.

SELF-STUDY *See page 85.*

Sales sense

PREPARE **A** Work in groups of four. Think of a product you would like to sell. On a separate piece of paper, write the name of your product and three ways you could use the senses to sell it.

Smooth Milk Chocolate

Sight: Use a bright red wrapper to make people feel happy.

Taste: Mix chocolate with unusual flavors like lemon and coconut.

Hearing: Use the sound of milk pouring into a glass in TV ads.

PRACTICE **B** 1. Listen and practice. Notice the pronunciation of the vowel sounds.

/æ/ = brand	/ɔː/ = soft	/e/ = sense	/oʊ/ = nose
/uː/ = smooth	/iː/ = sweet	/eɪ/ = taste	/ʌ/ = touch

2. Listen. Circle the words you hear.

a. shops / (shapes)
b. store / star

c. taste / test
d. fail / feel

e. eat / ate
f. shoes / shows

SPEAK **C** 1. Work with a partner. Tell your partner about your group's product. Use the information from Exercise A.

> Our product is called Smooth Milk Chocolate. We'll use a bright red wrapper . . .

2. Would you buy your partner's product? Why or why not?

> I'd definitely buy Smooth Milk Chocolate. I love lemon and coconut, and . . .

A Take the Dating Survey. Check (✓) your answers.

Dating Survey

	agree	disagree	not sure
1. I would trust my parents to choose a good partner for me.	☐	☐	☐
2. I would trust my friends to find a good partner for me.	☐	☐	☐
3. My first impressions of people are usually correct.	☐	☐	☐
4. A blind date is a good way to start a relationship.	☐	☐	☐
5. The Internet is a good place to find someone to date.	☐	☐	☐
6. People who meet through a matchmaker don't usually fall in love.	☐	☐	☐
7. A matchmaker is a good way to find the right partner.	☐	☐	☐
8. It's best to wait and fall in love by chance.	☐	☐	☐

B Work with a partner. Share your responses from Exercise A. Explain the reasons for your answers.

I would trust my parents to choose a good partner for me.
They know me very well and want me to be happy.

Which way is best?

A 🎧 **Listen. Students are talking about ways people meet and begin dating. Write one advantage and one disadvantage for each way.**

Ways to meet	Advantages	Disadvantages
1. being introduced through a matchmaker	*can find out about each other's backgrounds*	
2. being introduced by a friend or relative		
3. meeting by chance		

B 🎧 **Listen again. Who thinks it's a good way to meet and begin dating? Check (✓) *man*, *woman*, or *both*.**

	man	woman	both
1.	☐	☑	☐
2.	☐	☐	☐
3.	☐	☐	☐

How did they meet?

MAIN IDEA **A** 🎧 Listen. People are talking about their parents. Write how they met. Use the phrases in the box. (There are two extra phrases.)

☐ on a blind date	☐ through a friend	☐ through a sister
☑ by chance	☐ through a matchmaker	☐ through the woman's parents

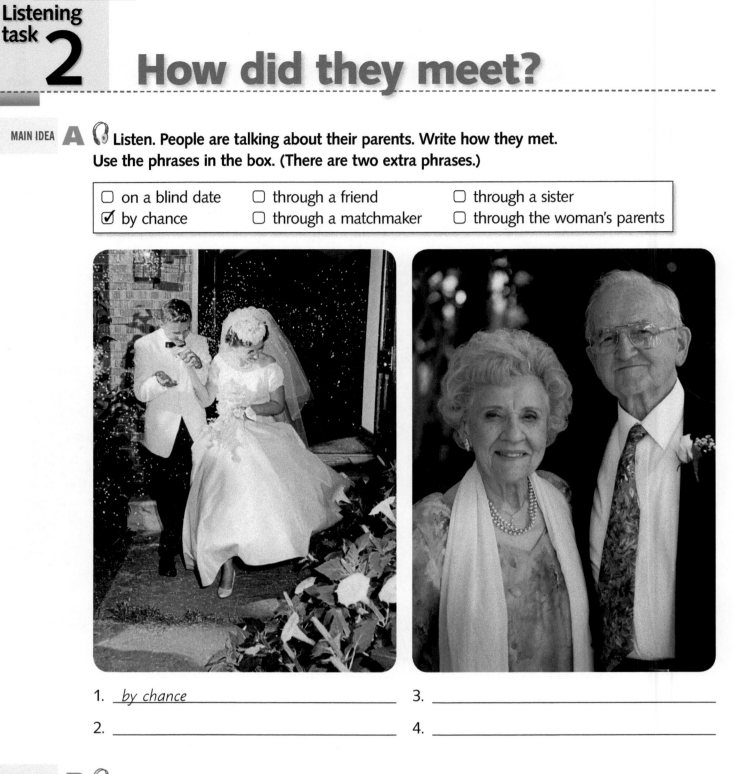

1. *by chance*   3. _____

2. _____   4. _____

DETAILS **B** 🎧 Listen again. What were their first impressions? Complete the sentences. Then check (✓) if their impressions are the same or different now.

	first impression	same	different
1. He was	*kind of shy* .	☐	☑
2. She was	_____ .	☐	☐
3. She was	_____ .	☐	☐
4. He was	_____ .	☐	☐

SELF-STUDY *See page 86.*

My best match

PREPARE **A** Think about dating. What is important to you in a partner? Add one idea to each
category. Then check (✓) five things that are important to you.

I want a partner who . . . .

Background
- ☐ has a good education
- ☐ has a good job
- ☐ has a lot of money
- ☐ is from a good family
- ☐ _____

Personality
- ☐ gets along with my family
- ☐ gets along with my friends
- ☐ has a similar personality
- ☐ _____

Appearance
- ☐ is handsome/beautiful
- ☐ is taller/shorter than I am
- ☐ _____

Interests
- ☐ likes the same things I do
- ☐ likes to travel
- ☐ studies English
- ☐ _____

PRACTICE **B** **1.** 🎧 **Listen and practice. Notice the intonation when saying lists.**

I'd like to meet someone who likes to play sports, travel, and study English.

I want a partner who gets along with my parents, my friends, and my dog.

I want a partner who has a good job, a good education, and similar interests.

2. 🎧 **Listen. Number the lists in the correct order from 1 to 3.**

a. ☐2 a good education   b. ☐ English   c. ☐ handsome   d. ☐ fell in love

☐1 a good job   ☐ French   ☐ tall   ☐ got married

☐3 a lot of money   ☐ Spanish   ☐ dark   ☐ met by chance

SPEAK **C** Work with a partner. Share your answers from Exercise A. Which qualities do
you agree are important?

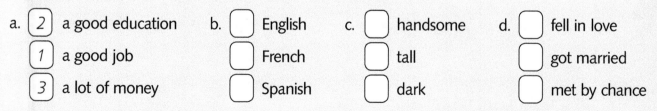

*I want a partner who has a good education, is handsome,
and gets along with my family.*

I want a partner who has a good education, too.

Warming up

A Look at the scene from a university class. Read the statements. Circle the ones you agree with.

Communication Differences

People should . . . .

- speak politely to older people
- apologize often, even for small mistakes
- touch each other while speaking
- use first names with most people

People shouldn't . . . .

- criticize others
- disagree with others
- give opinions directly
- interrupt the speaker

B Work with a partner. Talk about the statements you agree with from Exercise A. Give reasons.

> *I think people should speak politely to older people. It's important to show respect.*

I just don't understand.

MAIN IDEA **A** 🎧 **Listen. People are talking about communication misunderstandings. What are the topics? Circle the correct answers.**

1. a. interrupting
   b. *(giving opinions directly)*

2. a. apologizing
   b. speaking politely

3. a. criticizing
   b. interrupting

4. a. criticizing
   b. disagreeing with others

DETAILS **B** 🎧 **Listen again. What advice does each person give? Circle the correct information.**

1. If you think someone is wrong, *don't say anything* / *(ask a question)*.

2. Give a *reason* / *gift* only if you do something really bad.

3. Ask the person to *speak loudly* / *let you finish*.

4. Try to express yourself more *directly* / *indirectly*.

It's our style.

MAIN IDEA **A** 🎧 Listen. Students are talking about communication styles in their countries. Check (✓) the behaviors that are OK to do. Cross out (✗) the behaviors that are not OK.

Luis   Soon Jin   Ali

	Colombia	South Korea	Saudi Arabia
1. interrupting someone	✗	✗	✓
2. touching the other person	☐	☐	☐
3. disagreeing	☐	☐	☐
4. saying "no" directly	☐	☐	☐

DETAILS **B** 🎧 Listen again. Who makes these statements? Write *Luis, Soon Jin,* or *Ali.*

1. "It's best to wait until the other person finishes."   *Luis*

2. "I might touch him on the arm or the hand."   _____

3. "We are very direct when we disagree."   _____

4. "It's very important to respect your friends."   _____

Good communication

PREPARE **A** Work with a partner. Choose a culture you know well. What are five important communication tips for visitors to the culture? Complete the chart.

Communication Tips for Visitors

Behavior	Example of the behavior
You should be polite to older people.	_You shouldn't use first names._
1. _____	_____
2. _____	_____
3. _____	_____
4. _____	_____
5. _____	_____

PRACTICE **B** **1.** 🎧 Listen and practice. Notice that the *t* in final position in *shouldn't* is not strongly pronounced.

We shouldn't touch people when speaking.   You shouldn't use first names.
People shouldn't interrupt the speaker.   People shouldn't disagree directly.

2. 🎧 Listen. Do you hear *should* or *shouldn't*? Check (✓) the correct answers.

	should	shouldn't			should	shouldn't			should	shouldn't
a.	☑	☐		c.	☐	☐		e.	☐	☐
b.	☐	☐		d.	☐	☐		f.	☐	☐

SPEAK **C** **1.** Join another pair. Share your communication tips from Exercise A. Remember to give examples.

> You should be polite to older people. For example, you shouldn't use first names.

2. Make a list of your group's top five tips for good communication. Then share the list with the class.

Listening task 1 • Information

MAIN IDEA **A** 🎧 **Listen. People are talking about Russia. What are they talking about? Write the topics in the chart below.**

Red Square

RUSSIA: Fact File

Topics	Information		
1. _general information_	**Name (1922–1991)** _the U.S.S.R._	**Name today** _____ _____ _____	**Capital** _____
2. _____ _____	**Saint Petersburg** State Hermitage _____	**Moscow** • the _____ • _____ _____	
3. _____ _____	**Don't . . . .** • _____ _____ in a _____ • _____ when you _____ _____		
4. _____ _____	**When you introduce someone, ...** • use the person's _____ _____ • use first names only with _____ _____		

DETAILS **B** 🎧 **Listen again. Complete the missing information in the chart.**

Listening task 2 • Dating and marriage traditions

MAIN IDEA **A** 🎧 **Listen. A student is talking about dating and marriage traditions in the past. Complete the information. Then check (✓) if the traditions are the same or different now.**

	traditions in the past	traditions now same	different
1. where people met	*in college or university*	✓	☐
2. age when people married	_____	☐	☐
3. who people married	_____	☐	☐
4. what people did on a date	_____	☐	☐

DETAILS **B** 🎧 **Listen again. Are the statements true or false? Check (✓) the correct answers.**

	true	false
1. Russians used to have arranged marriages.	☐	✓
2. In the past, Russian women married earlier than men.	☐	☐
3. The woman and her husband have the same job.	☐	☐
4. Today, Russians hang out in cafés on a date.	☐	☐

Warming up

A Work with a partner. What do people use the Internet for? Write the activities from the box in the correct categories.

☑ buy gifts   ☐ do academic research   ☐ order concert tickets
☐ buy used goods   ☐ download music   ☐ read the news
☐ chat or instant-message   ☐ get local weather reports   ☐ take online classes
☐ check vacation plans   ☐ make airline reservations   ☐ write a blog

weblinks

communication
_____
_____

education
_____
_____

entertainment
_____
_____

travel
_____
_____

information
_____
_____

shopping
_buy gifts_____
_____

B Go around the class. What do your classmates use the Internet for?
Try to find one person who does each of the activities in Exercise A.

Do you ever use the Internet to buy gifts?

Yes, I buy gifts on the Internet a lot.

Great site!

INFERENCE **A** 🎧 Listen. Some friends are looking at a Web site. Number the links they visit from 1 to 5. (There is one extra link.)

INFERENCE **B** 🎧 Listen again. Who likes the links? Check (✓) *man* or *woman*. Then write the reasons.

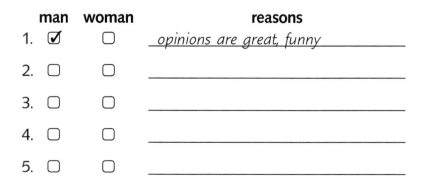

	man	woman	reasons
1.	✓	☐	*opinions are great, funny*
2.	☐	☐	_____
3.	☐	☐	_____
4.	☐	☐	_____
5.	☐	☐	_____

2 The growth of the Internet

DETAILS **A** 🎧 Listen. How has the Internet grown since it first started? Complete the missing information in the chart below.

	1990s	Today
1. number of users	• _16 million_	• _____
2. types of users	• _university students_ • _____	• _____ • _____
3. Internet access	• _offices_ • _____ • _____	• _____ • _____ • _____
4. Internet use	• _sell products and services_ • _____	• _____ • _____ • _____ • _____

DETAILS **B** 🎧 Listen again. What are the predictions for the future of the Internet? Complete the sentences.

1. The number of users around the world will _continue_ to _grow_ .

2. More and _____ people of _____ ages will enjoy the Internet.

3. Users will find _____ Internet access in even more _____ .

4. The computer will become an essential _____ in people's _____ .

SELF-STUDY *See page 88.*

My homepage

PREPARE **A** Design your own homepage. What features would you include? What would visitors be able to do there? Draw a picture of your homepage on a separate piece of paper.

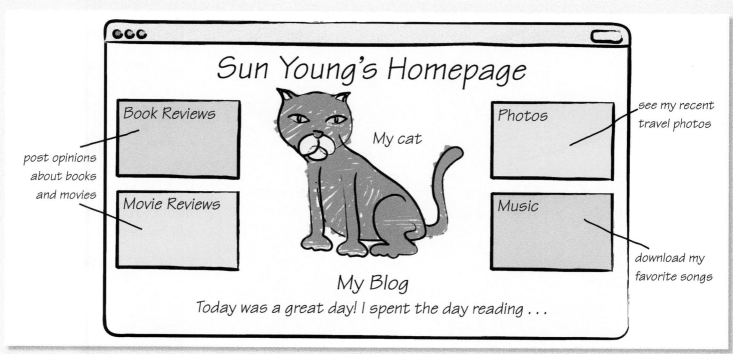

PRACTICE **B** **1.** 🎧 Listen and practice. Notice how the verbs link with words beginning with a vowel.

present	past
I save all my e-mail.	I saved all my e-mail.
The students love instant messages.	The students loved instant messages.

2. 🎧 Listen. Is the verb in the present or past? Check (✓) the correct answers.

	present	past		present	past		present	past
a.	✓	☐	c.	☐	☐	e.	☐	☐
b.	☐	☐	d.	☐	☐	f.	☐	☐

SPEAK **C** Work in groups of four. Describe your homepage from Exercise A. Take turns talking about each feature and what visitors can do there.

> *My homepage has book and movie reviews. Visitors can post opinions about books and movies.*

A Read the meanings these objects have in different cultures. Are they the same or different for you? Write *S* (same), *D* (different), or *N* (no special meaning).

☐ If you walk under a ladder, you'll have bad luck.

☐ The number seven is lucky.

☐ If a black cat walks in front of you, something bad will happen.

☐ If you stand chopsticks in a bowl of rice, you'll have bad luck.

☐ A broom behind the door will keep out unwanted visitors.

☐ Going out at night when there's a full moon is bad luck.

☐ Friday the thirteenth is an unlucky day.

☐ You'll have good luck if you see a white snake.

☐ Breaking a mirror will bring seven years of bad luck.

B Work with a partner. Compare your answers from Exercise A. Then think of three more superstitions you know and share them with the class.

Around the world

MAIN IDEA **A** 🎧 Listen. People are talking about superstitions. What countries have these superstitions? What do they mean? Complete the missing information.

Superstition	Country	Meaning
1. a black cat 	_the U.S._ _____	_have bad luck_ _____
2. a snake	_____ _____	_____ _____
3. a full moon	_____ _____	_____ _____
4. a broom	_____ _____	_____ _____

INFERENCE **B** 🎧 Listen again. Circle the correct answers.

1. The man *knew* / *didn't know* the Scottish superstition.

2. The woman *believes* / *doesn't believe* the Thai superstition.

3. When there's a full moon, the woman usually *goes out* / *stays home.*

4. The man thinks he is *lucky* / *unlucky.*

The real meaning

MAIN IDEA **A** 🎧 **Listen. People are talking about superstitious beliefs. What are the superstitions? Check (✓) the correct answers.**

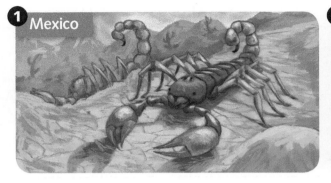

1 Mexico

When scorpions come down from the mountain, people say it will
- ☐ be hot.
- ☑ rain.

2 the U.K.

Never lend milk to anyone because the person might be a witch who will
- ☐ make your cow stop giving milk.
- ☐ steal your cow.

3 Brazil

Landowners told workers not to eat mangoes because they would
- ☐ get sick.
- ☐ lose their jobs.

4 Japan

If children don't cover their stomachs during a storm, the thunder god will steal
- ☐ their belly buttons.
- ☐ the children.

DETAILS **B** 🎧 **Listen again. What are the reasons for the superstitions? Complete the sentences.**

1. Scorpions can feel _the winds_ . The winds always blow _before it rains_ .

2. Most people were very _____ . They couldn't afford to _____ .

3. The landowners said that so the workers wouldn't _____ .

4. During a storm, the temperature _____ . They cover themselves so they

   won't _____ .

SELF-STUDY *See page 89.*

Are you superstitious?

PREPARE **A** Look at the game board. How superstitious are you? Read the questions and think about your answers.

ARE YOU SUPERSTITIOUS?

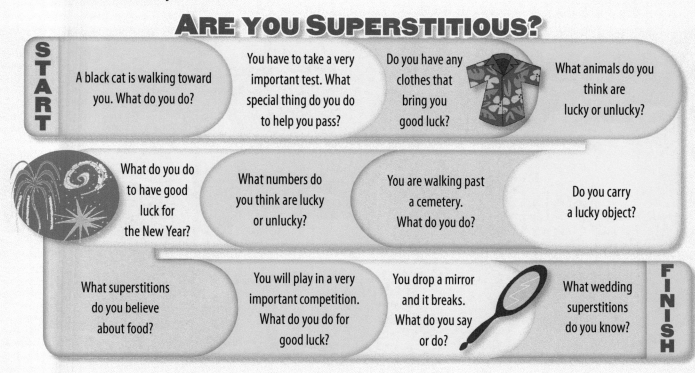

START

A black cat is walking toward you. What do you do?

You have to take a very important test. What special thing do you do to help you pass?

Do you have any clothes that bring you good luck?

What animals do you think are lucky or unlucky?

What do you do to have good luck for the New Year?

What numbers do you think are lucky or unlucky?

You are walking past a cemetery. What do you do?

Do you carry a lucky object?

What superstitions do you believe about food?

You will play in a very important competition. What do you do for good luck?

You drop a mirror and it breaks. What do you say or do?

What wedding superstitions do you know?

FINISH

PRACTICE **B** **1.** Listen and practice. Notice the regular rhythm of stressed words.

If you break a mirror, / you'll have seven years / of bad luck.
At New Year's, / we wear red clothes / for good luck.
People say a broom / behind the door / will keep out / unwanted visitors.

2. Underline the stressed words. Then listen and check your answers.

a. In some <u>places</u>, a black <u>cat</u> brings good <u>luck</u>.
b. Some people wear blue when they get married.
c. I always eat an orange before I take a test.
d. In my culture, people believe snakes are unlucky.

SPEAK **C** Play the game in Exercise A in groups of four. Put your markers on "Start." Flip a coin to move.

 Move one space.

 Move two spaces.

heads

tails

When you land on a space, your classmates ask you questions about that topic.

Warming up

A How do you feel about these situations? Check (✓) your answers.

	It doesn't bother me.	It bothers me a little.	It drives me crazy!
1. A person in the movie theater talks loudly during the movie.	☐	☐	☐
2. A friend arrives half an hour late to meet you for dinner at a restaurant.	☐	☐	☐
3. You send several e-mails to your friend, but she never responds.	☐	☐	☐
4. The person next to you on the bus talks on a cell phone nonstop.	☐	☐	☐
5. You are getting on the train. Someone pushes you away and takes the last seat.	☐	☐	☐

B Work with a partner. Compare your answers from Exercise A. Then think of two more situations that drive you crazy and share them with the class.

It drives me crazy!

MAIN IDEA **A** 🎧 Listen. People are talking about rude situations. Number the situations from 1 to 5. (There is one extra situation.)

INFERENCE **B** 🎧 Listen again. What would the people probably say about the situations? Check (✓) the correct answers.

	"It doesn't bother me."	"It bothers me a little."	"It drives me crazy!"
1.	☐	☐	☑
2.	☐	☐	☐
3.	☐	☐	☐
4.	☐	☐	☐
5.	☐	☐	☐

Mind your manners.

MAIN IDEA **A** 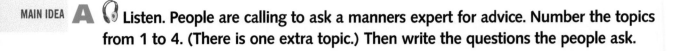 Listen. People are calling to ask a manners expert for advice. Number the topics from 1 to 4. (There is one extra topic.) Then write the questions the people ask.

Good Manners

Topics	Questions
☐ neighbors	_____ _____
1 dating	*Who pays for the date?* _____
☐ e-mail	_____ _____
☐ tipping	_____ _____
☐ wedding gifts	_____ _____

DETAILS **B** 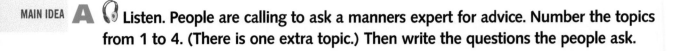 Listen again. What advice does the manners expert give? Write the expert's *Good Manners* tips.

1. *The person who invites should pay.*

2. _____

3. _____

4. _____

SELF-STUDY *See page 90.*

It really bothers me.

PREPARE **A** What situations drive you crazy? Write five things.

Situations That Drive Me Crazy

when people borrow things and don't return them

1.

2.

3.

4.

5.

PRACTICE **B** **1.** 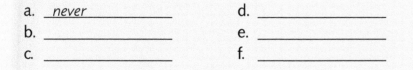 Listen and practice. Notice that some words are emphasized to express strong emotion.

I can't stand it when people are late.
It drives me crazy when people talk on cell phones.
My brother always talks during movies.
My sister never answers my e-mails.

2. Listen. Write the word that is emphasized to express strong emotion.

a. *never*   d. _____
b. _____   e. _____
c. _____   f. _____

SPEAK **C** Work in groups of four. Take turns sharing your responses from Exercise A. Your classmates will give their opinions.

> *It drives me crazy when people borrow things and don't return them.*

> *It drives me crazy, too!*

> *Yeah, I can't stand that either.*

Natural health

A Work with a partner. How much do you know about natural health remedies?
Match each remedy with its main health benefit. Then check your answers
on page 79.

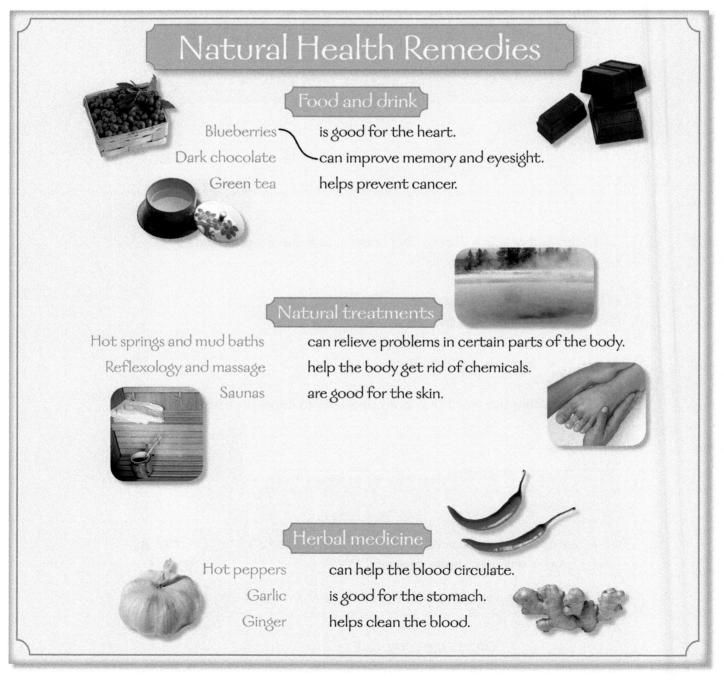

Natural Health Remedies

Food and drink

Blueberries — is good for the heart.

Dark chocolate ⌐ can improve memory and eyesight.

Green tea helps prevent cancer.

Natural treatments

Hot springs and mud baths can relieve problems in certain parts of the body.

Reflexology and massage help the body get rid of chemicals.

Saunas are good for the skin.

Herbal medicine

Hot peppers can help the blood circulate.

Garlic is good for the stomach.

Ginger helps clean the blood.

B Join another pair. Do you know any other natural health remedies and their benefits?
Write as many as you can on a separate piece of paper. Then share them with the class.

Reflexology

MAIN IDEA **A** 🎧 Listen. People are talking about the health benefits of reflexology. Number the areas of the feet from 1 to 5. (There are two extra areas.)

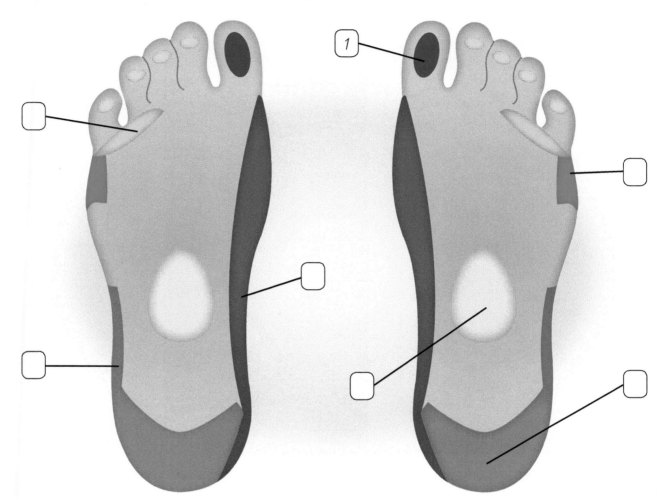

DETAILS **B** 🎧 Listen again. What health problems can reflexology help? Write the health problems.

1. _headaches_

2. _____

3. _____

4. _____

5. _____

Staying healthy

INFERENCE **A** 🎧 Listen. People are talking about natural health treatments. Which ones are they talking about? Write the treatments in the chart below. (There is one extra treatment.)

	Treatment	What people do	Health benefits
1. Finland	*sauna*	*sit in a hot room*	*gets rid of chemicals*
2. Thailand			
3. North America			
4. Asia			

DETAILS **B** 🎧 Listen again. What do people do? What are the health benefits? Complete the chart.

SELF-STUDY *See page 91.*

A day at my spa

Your turn
to talk

PREPARE **A** Work with a partner. Imagine you are going to open a health spa. Design a spa schedule with health treatments and their benefits. Complete the chart.

	A day at _Nature's Way_ Health Spa	A day at _____ Health Spa
Morning	*Breakfast* *fresh blueberries — improve memory* *green tea — prevents cancer*	
Afternoon	*sauna — gets rid of chemicals*	
Evening	*Thai massage — relaxes the body*	

PRACTICE **B** **1.** 🎧 Listen and practice. Notice the falling intonation at the end of thought groups.

Blueberries improve memory, and green tea prevents cancer.

Saunas are good for you because they help the body get rid of chemicals.

Massage is good in the evening because it relaxes the body and helps you sleep.

2. 🎧 Listen. Check (✓) the words that end the two thought groups in each sentence.

a. ☐ mud baths   b. ☐ garlic   c. ☐ pain   d. ☐ tourists
   ☑ skin   ☐ blood   ☐ people   ☐ pain
   ☑ stress   ☐ stomach   ☐ relax   ☐ stress

SPEAK **C** **1.** Tell the class about your health spa from Exercise A. Talk about the treatments you will use and their health benefits.

> *We will have fresh blueberries and green tea for breakfast.*
> *Blueberries improve memory, and green tea prevents cancer.*

2. Take a class vote. Which spa do most people in the class want to try?

Listening task 1 • Information

MAIN IDEA **A**  Listen. People are talking about Ireland. What are they talking about? Write the topics in the chart below.

IRELAND: Fact File

Topics	Information		
1. *general information*	**Nickname** *the Emerald Isle*	**Capital** _____	**Languages** • *Irish (Gaelic)* • _____
2. _____ _____	**Trinity College** founded in _____	**Blarney Castle** home of the Blarney _____	
3. _____ _____	**Sports** • _____ • _____	**Music** • _____ _____ music • _____ music • famous group: _____	
4. _____	**Rude behaviors** • _____ • _____	**Topics to avoid** • _____ • _____	

DETAILS **B** Listen again. Complete the missing information in the chart.

Listening task 2 • Superstitions

INFERENCE **A** 🎧 **Listen. A student is talking about superstitions. Are the superstitions lucky or unlucky? Check (✓) the correct answers. Then write the words that gave you the hints.**

a horseshoe

the Blarney Stone

a red-haired woman

spilling salt

	lucky	unlucky	
1. hanging a horseshoe	☑	☐	_will bring health, happiness_ _good symbol_
2. kissing the Blarney Stone	☐	☐	_____ _____
3. spilling salt	☐	☐	_____ _____
4. seeing a red-haired woman before fishing	☐	☐	_____ _____

DETAILS **B** 🎧 **Listen again. What do people believe about the superstitions? Complete the sentences with the missing information.**

1. If you hang a horseshoe upside down, _the luck will run out_____ .

2. Kissing the stone _____ .

3. If you spill salt, _____ .

4. If a fisherman saw a red-haired woman, he _____ .

Unit 9

Science trivia

Warming up

A Work with a partner. Can you guess the answers to the Science Trivia Quiz?
Circle your guesses.

Science Trivia Quiz

1. *Cold / Hot* water freezes faster.

2. *Mosquitoes / Tigers* are more dangerous to humans.

3. Light from the sun reaches the earth in eight *seconds / minutes*.

4. A strawberry looks red because it *absorbs / reflects* light.

5. A *man's / woman's* sense of smell is stronger.

6. In a lifetime, humans *have more heartbeats / take more breaths*.

7. *Adults / Babies* have more bones.

8. Spiders have been used to treat *baldness / toothaches*.

B Join another pair. Compare answers. Then check your answers on page 79.

Fact or fiction?

DETAILS **A** Listen. Friends are playing a science game. What scientific beliefs are they talking about? Complete the sentences.

Bats *are really blind* _____ .

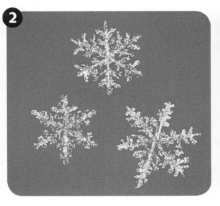

No two snowflakes _____ _____ .

Bee stings are used _____ _____ .

Boiled water _____ _____ .

Full moons _____ _____ .

You can catch a cold by being _____ .

DETAILS **B** Listen again. Are the beliefs true, false, or unknown? Check (✓) the correct answers. Then write the reasons.

	true	false	unknown	reasons
1.	☐	☑	☐	*aren't blind, have the ability to see*
2.	☐	☐	☐	
3.	☐	☐	☐	
4.	☐	☐	☐	
5.	☐	☐	☐	
6.	☐	☐	☐	

The northern lights

MAIN IDEA **A** 🎧 Listen. A woman is talking about the northern lights. What is she talking about? Number the topics below from 1 to 5. (There is one extra topic.)

Topics	best place	areas
☐ places to see the lights	• _____ _____	• _____ • _____ • _____
	name	country
☐ the discovery of the lights	• _____	• _____
	colors	shapes
☐ 1 a description of the lights	• _green, red,_ _____	• _____ • _____ • _____
	Finnish	Inuit
☐ beliefs about the lights	• _____ _____	• _____ _____
	language	*aurora* means
☐ the meaning of *aurora borealis*	• _____	• _____ *borealis* means • _____
	similar to	cause
☐ the scientific explanation for the lights	• _____	• _____ particles (electrons) collide with _____ atoms.

DETAILS **B** 🎧 Listen again. Complete the missing information in the chart.

SELF-STUDY *See page 92.*

Trivia game

PREPARE **A** Work with a partner. Student A, use this page. Student B, turn to page 78.
Don't show your page to your classmates! Read the trivia questions and
try to guess the missing answers.

Science Trivia Game

What is the longest river
on Earth?
the Nile River

Are Europe and North America moving
closer together or farther apart?
_____

Which is deeper: the Atlantic Ocean
or the Pacific Ocean?
_____

What is another name for the
symbol 0_2?
_____

How many times per second
does a fly beat its wings?
three hundred and thirty times

TRUE or FALSE?
Frogs breathe through their skin.
_____

TRUE or FALSE?
Many years ago, some people
thought the earth was flat.
_____

Where is the oldest mountain
range on Earth?
Scotland

How many planets are there in
the earth's solar system?
nine

PRACTICE **B** 1. Listen and practice. Notice the different pronunciations of *th*.

th = /θ/	th = /ð/

thirty	their
something	farther
Earth	breathe
_____	_another_
_____	_____
_____	_____

2. Write the words in the correct columns. Then listen and check your answers.

✓another	breath	northern	south	thought	together

SPEAK **C** Play the game in Exercise A with the class. Go around the room and ask classmates
the questions. Write the missing answers on the game board.

Excuse me. What is the longest river on Earth?   _It's the Nile River._

Advertising

A Work with a partner. What are some companies that are known for these products? Write two companies for each product.

cars

clothing and accessories

credit cards

_____

_____

snack foods

soft drinks

sportswear

_____

_____

B Which companies use these things in their ads? Write companies from Exercise A and other companies you know in the correct columns.

Beautiful people	Celebrities	Humor	Songs or slogans	Strong emotions

What's in a name?

DETAILS A 🎧 Listen. These American companies used to have different names. Match the original company names with their logos. (There are four extra names.)

a. Baked Foods
b. Bank Americard
c. Canning International
d. Citibank North America
e. Consolidated Foods Corporation
f. Minnesota Valley Canning Company
g. Mobil
h. Standard Oil

❶ VISA ☐

❷ Sara Lee ☐

❸ ExxonMobil ☐

❹ Green Giant ☐

DETAILS B 🎧 Listen again. Why did the companies change their names? Circle the correct answers.

1. The company wanted to
   a. offer passport services.
   b. become international.

2. The company
   a. began making baked goods.
   b. wanted a well-known name.

3. The company wanted a name that was
   a. original and different.
   b. similar to its original name.

4. The company was named for
   a. a type of vegetable.
   b. the King of England.

Lost in translation

MAIN IDEA **A** 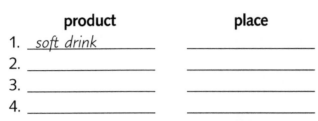 Listen. People are talking about problems advertising companies have had in different parts of the world. Write the product and the place for each problem.

	product	place
1.	*soft drink*	
2.		
3.		
4.		

DETAILS **B** Listen again. What were the problems? Complete the sentences.

1. The slogan was "_Come alive!_"
   It was translated as "Bring ancestors _____."

2. Languages are written _____ .
   People thought the product would make clothes _____ .

3. The first word should have been "_____."
   The slogan was translated as "_____ I wore this shirt, I felt good."

4. The company was unsuccessful because of its _____ .
   It means "_____" in Japanese.

SELF-STUDY *See page 93.*

It's a great product.

PREPARE **A** Work in groups of three. Choose a product you would like to advertise. Write your advertising plan on a separate piece of paper. Then write a script for a brief TV or radio ad.

Advertising plan	
Company name *Fantastic Fashions*	**Product name** *Perfect Fit jeans*
Celebrities or people in ad *the students in the class*	**Slogan** *"You can feel perfect with Perfect Fit jeans."*

> *I'm wearing Perfect Fit jeans from Fantastic Fashions. I feel perfect! You can feel perfect, too, with Perfect Fit jeans . . .*

PRACTICE **B** **1.** Listen and practice. Notice the pronunciation of vowel sounds followed by *r*.

/ɜr/	/er/	/ɑr/	/ɔːr/
advertise perfect (adj.)	compare wear	large smart	warm more
commercial			

2. Write these words in the correct columns. Then listen and check your answers.

> ✓ commercial   dirty   market   pair   scare   sports   star   store

SPEAK **C** Join another group. Perform your ads from Exercise A. The other group tells which aspects of the ad would make them buy your product. Then change roles.

> *I would buy Perfect Fit jeans. The name makes them sound comfortable.*

> *Me, too. I like . . .*

A Imagine that you want to study English in another country. What is important to you? Take the Study Abroad Survey. Check (✓) your choices, or write your own answers.

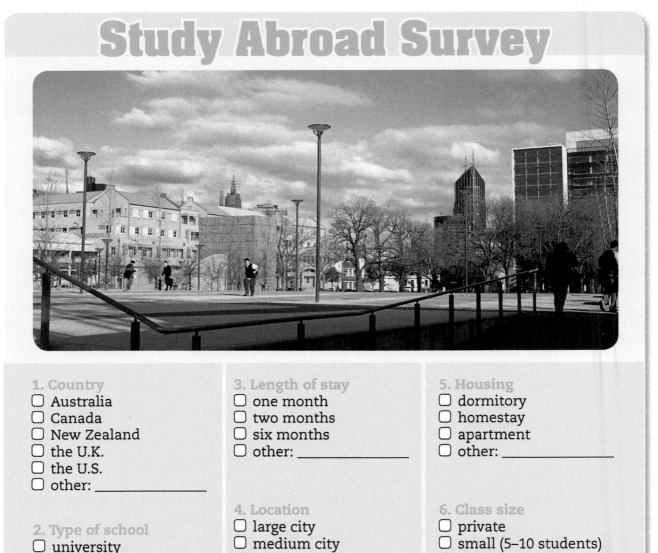

Study Abroad Survey

1. Country
- ☐ Australia
- ☐ Canada
- ☐ New Zealand
- ☐ the U.K.
- ☐ the U.S.
- ☐ other: _____

2. Type of school
- ☐ university
- ☐ private language school
- ☐ other: _____

3. Length of stay
- ☐ one month
- ☐ two months
- ☐ six months
- ☐ other: _____

4. Location
- ☐ large city
- ☐ medium city
- ☐ small town
- ☐ other: _____

5. Housing
- ☐ dormitory
- ☐ homestay
- ☐ apartment
- ☐ other: _____

6. Class size
- ☐ private
- ☐ small (5–10 students)
- ☐ large (over 10 students)
- ☐ other: _____

B Work with a partner. Compare your answers to the survey from Exercise A.

> *I'd like to go to Canada to study. I would stay . . .*

A place to live

MAIN IDEA **A** 🎧 Listen. Two friends are talking about housing choices for studying abroad. Number the choices from 1 to 5. (There is one extra choice.)

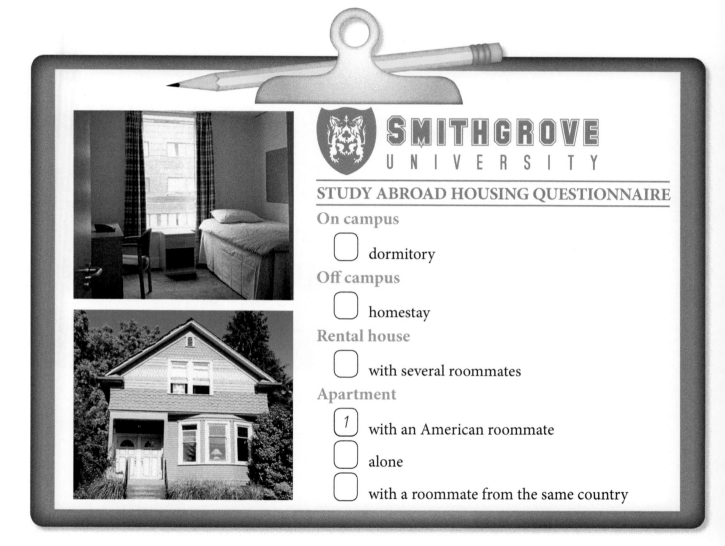

SMITHGROVE
U N I V E R S I T Y

STUDY ABROAD HOUSING QUESTIONNAIRE

On campus
☐ dormitory

Off campus
☐ homestay

Rental house
☐ with several roommates

Apartment
[1] with an American roommate
☐ alone
☐ with a roommate from the same country

DETAILS **B** 🎧 Listen again. Write one advantage and one disadvantage for each choice in Exercise A.

	advantages	disadvantages
1.	help improve English	difficulty communicating
2.		
3.		
4.		
5.		

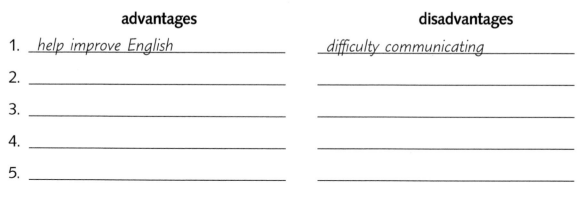

Listening task 2 Choosing a school

MAIN IDEA A 🎧 Listen. A professor is talking to a student about features of a study abroad program in Australia. Complete the missing information.

1. location   _near Sydney_____

2. type of school   _____

3. length of stay   _____ weeks or _____ weeks

4. class size   _____

5. housing   _____

INFERENCE B 🎧 Listen again. Does the professor like the features? Check (✓) *yes* or *no*. Then write the words that gave you the hints.

	yes	no	
1.	☑	☐	_quiet, convenient, perfect for a student_
2.	☐	☐	_____
3.	☐	☐	_____
4.	☐	☐	_____
5.	☐	☐	_____

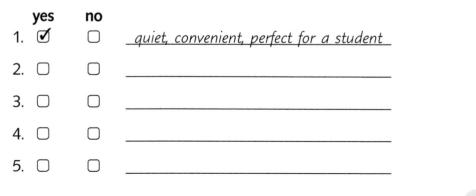

52   **Unit 11** Study abroad   SELF-STUDY *See page 94.*

The perfect school

PREPARE **A** Work with a partner. Imagine you are going to open your own English school. Design your school's brochure on a separate piece of paper.

Aloha English Center

Location
Waikiki Beach, Hawaii, U.S.A.
School is next to the beach.

Housing
homestay or dormitory

Length of stay
2 weeks, 2 months, or 2 years

Class size
private and small group

Other information
Students can take surfing lessons.

PRACTICE **B** **1.**  Listen and practice. Notice the intonation of tag questions.

Living with a roommate would be cheaper, wouldn't it?

The dorms aren't too far from campus, are they?

The school is near the train station, isn't it?

You don't offer private classes, do you?

2. Listen. Check (✓) the tag questions you hear.

a. ☑ aren't they?
   ☐ don't they?

b. ☐ is it?
   ☐ was it?

c. ☐ do you?
   ☐ don't you?

d. ☐ isn't she?
   ☐ doesn't she?

e. ☐ would I?
   ☐ do I?

f. ☐ is it?
   ☐ doesn't it?

SPEAK **C** **1.** Join another pair. Read each other's brochures from Exercise A. Then ask your classmates questions to find out which school is best for you.

> The teachers are native speakers, aren't they?

2. Tell the class which English school you would choose and why.

> I would choose Aloha English Center because students can take surfing lessons.

A How much do you rely on modern technology? Take the Modern Technology Survey. Write your answers.

Modern Technology Survey

1. How many electrical appliances do you use each day? _____

2. What electronic devices do you use for work or school? _____

3. What do you sometimes buy from vending machines? _____

4. What's an electronic device you would like to own? _____

5. How many cell phones have you owned? _____

6. What electronic devices could you not live without? _____

7. Do you own a car with a Global Positioning System (GPS)? _____

8. Do you use a personal digital assistant (PDA)? _____

B Work with a partner. Compare your answers to the survey. Who uses the most appliances and devices?

Electronic devices

INFERENCE **A** 🎧 **Listen. People are talking about electronic devices. What are the different parts? Label the pictures with the correct parts from the box.**

☐ digital signal processor	☐ keypad	☐ playlist	☐ satellites
☐ flash memory	☑ LCD screen	☐ radio waves	☐ stylus
☐ image sensor	☐ microprocessor	☐ GPS receiver	☐ touch screen

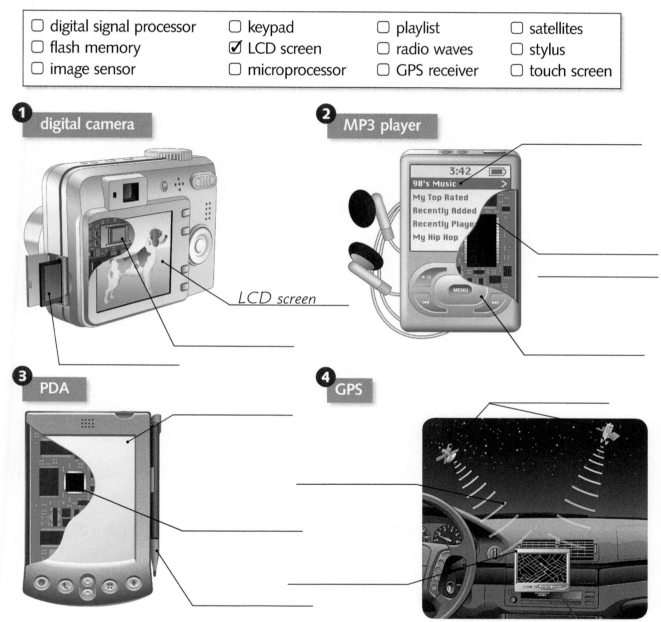

① digital camera

LCD screen

② MP3 player

③ PDA

④ GPS

MAIN IDEA **B** 🎧 **Listen again. Complete the sentences with the correct parts.**

1. The _____ stores the pictures.

2. The _____ displays the songs.

3. The _____ retrieves and stores information.

4. _____ send radio waves.

How a vending machine works

MAIN IDEA **A** 🎧 Listen. How does a vending machine work? What does it check for in each step? Complete the phrases.

Step 1: what _____ of _____ the coin is made of

Step 2: how _____ the coin _____

Step 3: how _____ or _____ the coin is

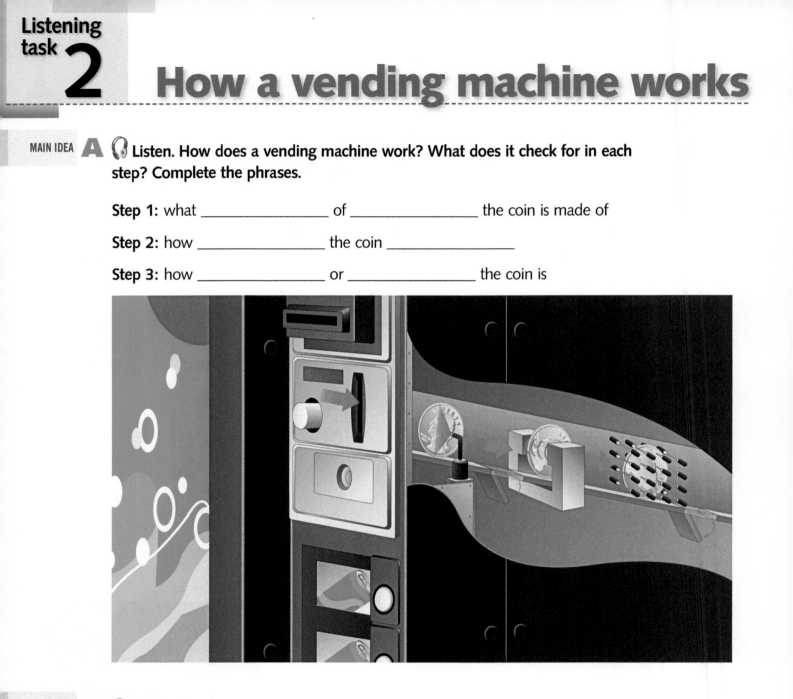

DETAILS **B** 🎧 Listen again. When do these things happen? Write *1* (Step 1), *2* (Step 2), or *3* (Step 3). (There is one extra item.)

_____ Lights check the color of the coin.

_____ The coin goes between two ends of the magnet.

_____ The coin passes between two sets of lights.

_1_ The coin in the money slot goes down a chute.

_____ A magnetic field slows down the coin.

_1_ Electricity passes through the coin.

_____ Lights measure the size of the coin.

 SELF-STUDY *See page 95.*

Here are the steps!

PREPARE **A** Work with a partner. Complete the chart with the names of appliances and devices
you use. Then describe how they work. Write three steps.

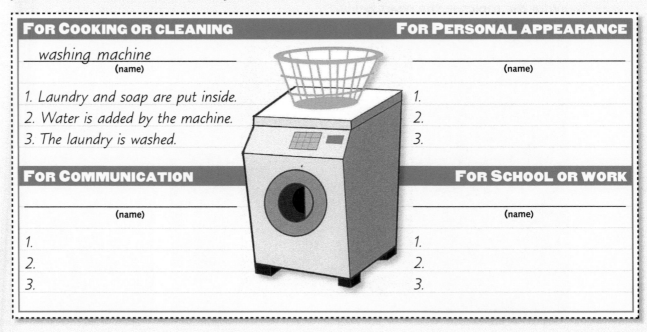

FOR COOKING OR CLEANING	FOR PERSONAL APPEARANCE
washing machine (name)	 (name)
1. Laundry and soap are put inside. 2. Water is added by the machine. 3. The laundry is washed.	1. 2. 3.

FOR COMMUNICATION	FOR SCHOOL OR WORK
  (name)	 (name)
1. 2. 3.	1. 2. 3.

PRACTICE **B** **1.** 🎧 **Listen and practice. Notice the reduction of *is* and *are* in rapid speech.**

The person's message is recorded.
If the coin is the correct size, it is accepted.

The pictures are saved in the flash memory.
Microprocessors are used in most computers.

2. 🎧 **Listen. Do you hear the reduction of *is* or *are*? Check (✓) the correct answers.**

	is	are		is	are		is	are
a.	☐	☑	c.	☐	☐	e.	☐	☐
b.	☐	☐	d.	☐	☐	f.	☐	☐

SPEAK **C** Join another pair. Take turns reading your steps from Exercise A.
Your classmates will try to guess the appliance or device.

> *Laundry and soap are put inside. Water is added by the machine.*

> *Is it a washing machine?*

> *Yes, that's right!*

Listening task 1 • Information

MAIN IDEA **A** Listen. People are talking about Brazil. What are they talking about?
Write the topics in the chart below.

BRAZIL: Fact File

Topics	Information		
1. *general information*	**Name origin** *brazilwood tree*	**Capital** _____	**Language** _____
2. _____	**Famous beaches** Copacabana and Ipanema, _____ in _____	**National sport** _____	**Famous festival** _____ held in _____
3. _____	**the Amazon River** • _____ river in the world • _____ percent of world's fresh water	**the Amazon Rain Forest** • annual rainfall: _____ millimeters • 2,000 types of _____ and _____	
4. _____	**Academic year** _____ to _____	**Study abroad** • _____ students every year • destinations include _____ , _____ , and _____	

DETAILS **B** Listen again. Complete the missing information in the chart.

Listening task 2 • Study abroad

MAIN IDEA **A** 🎧 **Listen. A student is talking about studying English in the U.S. How is the U.S. school different from her school in Brazil? Write the differences.**

	Brazil	the U.S.
1. type of school	*private college*	*university*
2. location		
3. class size		
4. other students		
5. housing		

DETAILS **B** 🎧 **Listen again. Which place does the woman prefer? Check (✓) the correct answers. Then write the reasons.**

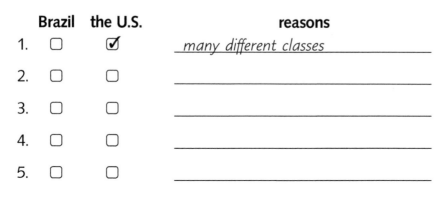

	Brazil	the U.S.	reasons
1.	☐	☑	*many different classes*
2.	☐	☐	
3.	☐	☐	
4.	☐	☐	
5.	☐	☐	

A Work with a partner. Read the personality traits associated with these blood types. Then match the descriptions with words from the box.

☐ cautious	☐ extroverted	☐ loyal	☐ picky
☑ competitive	☐ indecisive	☐ optimistic	☑ reserved
☐ confident	☐ independent	☑ organized	☑ sensitive

Blood types	Personality traits	
Type A	• good at planning things, likes things to be neat	*organized*
	• careful, avoids dangerous situations	
	• has a hard time making decisions	
Type AB	• doesn't show emotions or talk about problems	*reserved*
	• reliable, always ready to help a friend	
	• difficult to make happy, dislikes a lot of things	
Type B	• understands others' feelings	*sensitive*
	• doesn't like to ask others for help	
	• believes good things will happen in the future	
Type O	• always wants to be successful, likes to be the best	*competitive*
	• believes strongly in oneself	
	• enjoys being with other people	

B What is your blood type? Do the traits for your blood type in Exercise A match your personality? Tell the class.

It's in my blood.

MAIN IDEA **A** 🎧 Listen. People are talking about blood types and personalities. Write each person's blood type.

INFERENCE **B** 🎧 Listen again. Do the people think the blood types match their personalities? Check (✓) *yes* or *no*. Then write the words that gave you the hints.

	yes	no	
1.	✓	☐	*have to agree*
2.	☐	☐	_____
3.	☐	☐	_____
4.	☐	☐	_____
5.	☐	☐	_____
6.	☐	☐	_____

2 The Chinese zodiac

DETAILS **A** 🎧 Listen. People are describing the animals in the Chinese zodiac. Number three animals in the zodiac for each description.

extroverted

DETAILS **B** 🎧 Listen again. What personality traits do the animals have? Write one trait for each animal. Some traits are used more than once.

SELF-STUDY *See page 96.*

My personality traits

PREPARE **A** Choose three personality traits that describe you. Then write a hint for each trait on a separate piece of paper.

cautious	confident	indecisive	loyal	organized	reserved
competitive	extroverted	independent	optimistic	picky	sensitive

I'm optimistic, reserved, and picky.

	I always think good things will happen.
	I don't like showing my emotions.
	It's difficult to make me happy.

PRACTICE **B 1.** 🎧 Listen and practice. Notice the stressed syllables.

cautious   sensitive   competitive   optimistic   reserved

2. 🎧 Circle the stressed syllables. Then listen and check your answers.

a. (con)fident   c. picky   e. relaxed
b. emotional   d. independent f. indecisive

SPEAK **C 1. Work in groups of four. Read your hints from Exercise A. Can your classmates guess your personality traits?**

*I always think good things will happen.
I don't like showing my emotions . . .*

You're optimistic, reserved, . . .

2. Which personality traits do you have in common with your classmates? Can you guess each other's blood types or Chinese zodiac signs?

*Paul, you're really organized.
Are you blood type A?*

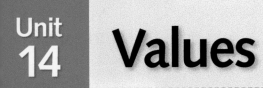

Warming up

A What do you think is important in today's society? Read the list below.
Then add two ideas of your own.

What's important?

☐ a clean environment
☐ having a career
☐ having enough money
☐ helping other people
☐ keeping old traditions and customs

☐ a relaxed lifestyle
☐ safety
☐ technology
☐ _____
☐ _____

B Work with a partner. Check (✓) the five most important things to you in Exercise A.

C Join another pair. Compare your lists. Explain your choices.

We think a clean environment is the most important thing. If the environment is clean, people have a better life.

Our first choice was technology. We think . . .

Difficult decisions

MAIN IDEA **A** 🎧 **Listen. People are talking about difficult decisions. They discuss the two positive points for each decision. Complete the missing information.**

1

marry Sam	OR	marry Brian
+ *nice guy*		+ *love each other*
+ *good job*		+ *same interests*

2

use the money for his daughter's private college	OR	use the money for his mother's nursing home
+ _____		+ _____
+ _____		+ _____

3

work for a large company	OR	work for a small company
+ _____		+ _____
+ _____		+ _____

4

study business	OR	study art
+ _____		+ _____
+ _____		+ _____

INFERENCE **B** 🎧 **Listen again. Which decisions will they probably make? Complete the phrases.**

1. marry *Brian* _____

2. use the money for _____

3. work for _____

4. study _____

Who's right?

MAIN IDEA **A**  **Listen. People are debating an important issue on a radio talk show. What are they talking about? Number the topics from 1 to 5. (There is one extra topic.)**

____ tourism and jobs   ____ environment and wildlife   ____ noise and crowds
____ subways and buses   ____ support for the change   _1_ the island's beauty

INFERENCE **B** **Listen again. Who probably agrees with these statements? Write *J* (Joyce), *R* (Robert), or *B* (both).**

Joyce Selles   Robert Williams

1. _B_ The island is a good place to live.

2. ____ Developing the island will help the people.

3. ____ The relaxed island lifestyle will be gone.

4. ____ Pollution may be a problem.

5. ____ The change will definitely happen.

SELF-STUDY *See page 97.*

Values game

PREPARE **A** Read the statements on the game board. Decide whether you agree or disagree. Then think of a sentence to explain your opinion.

A college education will help you get a better job.

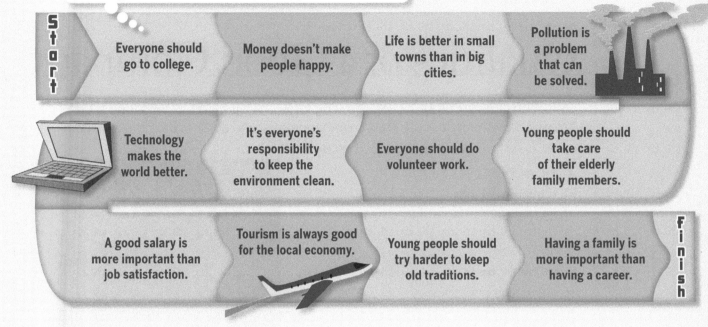

Start

| Everyone should go to college. | Money doesn't make people happy. | Life is better in small towns than in big cities. | Pollution is a problem that can be solved. |

| Technology makes the world better. | It's everyone's responsibility to keep the environment clean. | Everyone should do volunteer work. | Young people should take care of their elderly family members. |

| A good salary is more important than job satisfaction. | Tourism is always good for the local economy. | Young people should try harder to keep old traditions. | Having a family is more important than having a career. |

finish

PRACTICE **B** **1.** Listen and practice. Notice that *p, b, t, d, k,* and *g* are unreleased when followed by another consonant.

Education is very important to me.
Do you think pollution is a big problem?

People should try hard to keep customs.
You shouldn't take your job too seriously.

2. Circle the unreleased consonants in these sentences. Then listen and check your answers.

a. I think people should protect animals.
b. Do you think computers are necessary?

c. I would move to the city to find a job.
d. We need to work to keep traditions.

SPEAK **C** Play the game in Exercise A in groups of four. Put your markers on "Start." Flip a coin to move.

 Move one space.

 Move two spaces.

heads

tails

When you land on a space, your classmates ask you questions about that topic.

A What are the qualities of a good company? Circle five qualities in the magazine article that you think are important.

Qualities of a Good Company

What qualities are most important to employees? What makes a company a good place to work? We interviewed 100 company employees, and here are their top answers.

Type of business
• has interesting jobs
• helps people

Salary
• pays employees fairly
• gives regular pay raises

Benefits
• offers health insurance
• gives a lot of vacation time
• offers an opportunity to travel

Schedule and work environment
• treats employees with respect
• allows a balance of work and family life

Business principles
• cares about customer satisfaction
• has high standards for products and services
• is socially responsible
  - gives money to charity
  - cares about the environment

B Share your choices from Exercise A with the class. How many classmates agree with your choices?

The company has interesting jobs, pays employees . . .

The secret to success

MAIN IDEA **A**  Listen. People are talking about business advice. What is the best advice they have ever received? Complete the sentences.

1. Do *what you love to do* .

2. Don't _____ .

3. Try to _____ .

4. Respect _____ .

DETAILS **B** Listen again. Who gave them the advice? When did they receive it? Write the information.

who	when
1. *his grandmother*	*when he was ten years old*
2.	
3.	
4.	

Unit 15 Good business **69**

A success story

MAIN IDEA **A** 🎧 Listen. A man is talking about Starbucks Corporation. What are the company's six guiding business principles? Number the principles from 1 to 6.

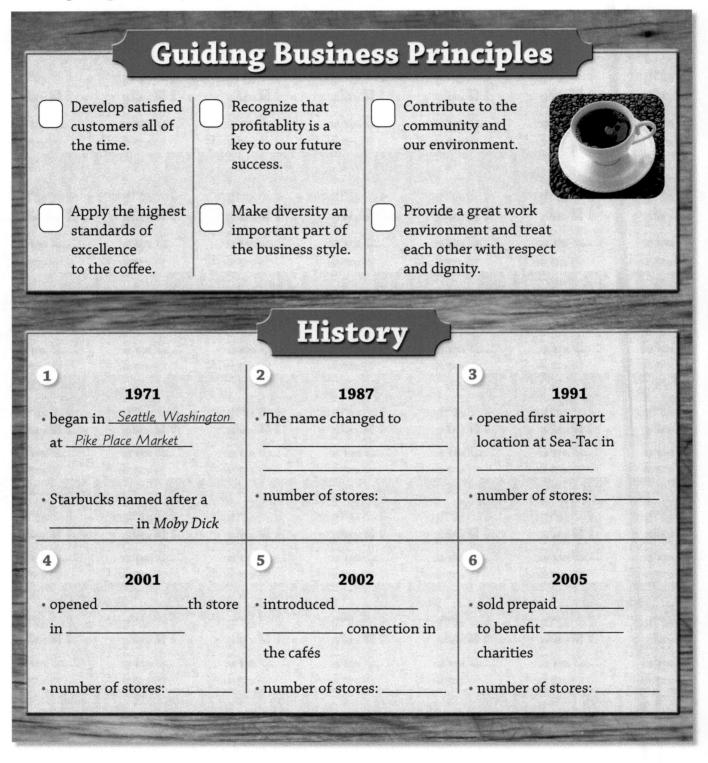

Guiding Business Principles

◻ Develop satisfied customers all of the time.

◻ Recognize that profitablity is a key to our future success.

◻ Contribute to the community and our environment.

◻ Apply the highest standards of excellence to the coffee.

◻ Make diversity an important part of the business style.

◻ Provide a great work environment and treat each other with respect and dignity.

History

1
1971
• began in _Seattle, Washington_ at _Pike Place Market_

• Starbucks named after a _____ in *Moby Dick*

2
1987
• The name changed to _____ _____

• number of stores: _____

3
1991
• opened first airport location at Sea-Tac in _____

• number of stores: _____

4
2001
• opened _____th store in _____

• number of stores: _____

5
2002
• introduced _____ _____ connection in the cafés

• number of stores: _____

6
2005
• sold prepaid _____ to benefit _____ charities

• number of stores: _____

DETAILS **B** 🎧 Listen again. Complete the missing information about Starbucks in the chart.

SELF-STUDY *See page 98.*

Company principles

PREPARE **A** Work in groups of four. Imagine you are starting your own company. What will
be your company's guiding principles? Write five principles for your company.

Company Principles

Make customer satisfaction an important goal.

1. _____

2. _____

3. _____

4. _____

5. _____

PRACTICE **B** **1.** 🎧 **Listen and practice. Notice the reduction of *to*.**

to = /tə/

Customer satisfaction is important to them.
We'll provide the opportunity to travel.
We plan to contribute a lot of money to charity.
We'd like to give people a chance to share ideas.

2. 🎧 **Listen. Do you hear one or two reductions of *to*? Check (✓) the correct answers.**

	one	two		one	two		one	two
a.	✓	☐	c.	☐	☐	e.	☐	☐
b.	☐	☐	d.	☐	☐	f.	☐	☐

SPEAK **C** Share your company principles from Exercise A with the class. Which group's company
would be the best place to work? Take a class vote.

One business principle is to make customer satisfaction an important goal. Another . . .

Unsolved mysteries

A Work with a partner. Do you know these mysterious things? Write the words in the correct columns below. Then check your answers on page 79.

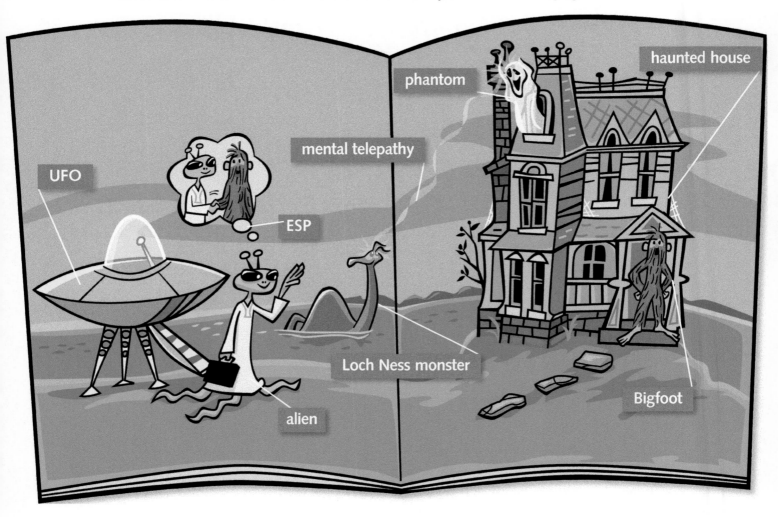

Ghosts	Life in outer space	Mysterious creatures	Psychic abilities

B What other mysterious things do you know? Write as many as you can on a separate piece of paper. Then share your answers with the class.

Strange stories

INFERENCE **A** 🎧 **Listen. People are telling strange stories. Which book or magazine does each story come from? Number the covers from 1 to 4. (There is one extra cover.)**

DETAILS **B** 🎧 **Listen again. Number the sentences in the correct order from 1 to 3.**

1. _____ I noticed something moving
   in the water.

   _____ It disappeared under the water.

   _____ We were returning to London.

2. _____ We tried to drive away.

   _____ We stopped the car to get
   a better look.

   _____ We woke up still sitting in
   the car.

3. _____ He opened the door.

   _____ He saw a woman standing there.

   _____ He woke us up around midnight.

4. _____ I was sitting up in bed
   and screaming.

   _____ It was my mother on the phone.

   _____ Around 3:00 A.M., I fell asleep.

MAIN IDEA **A** 🎧 **Listen. A researcher is answering questions about the mystery of crop circles. What questions does he answer? Number the questions below from 1 to 5. (There is one extra question.)**

questions	answers
_____ When are crop circles made?	_____
_____ What do people believe about crop circles?	_____
_____ Who or what makes the crop circles?	_____
_1_ What are crop circles?	*strange pictures, patterns in fields*
_____ When were the circles discovered?	_____
_____ Where are they found?	_____

DETAILS **B** 🎧 **Listen again. Write the researcher's answers to the questions.**

SELF-STUDY *See page 99.*

Believe it or not!

A Work with a partner. Create a television news story about a mysterious event in your community. Complete the chart.

NIGHTLY NEWS REPORT			
QUESTIONS	*ANSWERS*	*QUESTIONS*	*ANSWERS*
What happened?	*looked out my bedroom window and saw a giant crop circle*	What happened?	
When did it happen?	*7:30 yesterday morning*	When did it happen?	
Where did it happen?	*neighbor's garden*	Where did it happen?	
Who was there?	*two aliens, my neighbor, and his wife*	Who was there?	
What did you do?	*went back to bed*	What did you do?	

B **1.** Listen and practice. Notice that transition expressions are emphasized.

I thought it was an airplane, but then I saw the aliens.
I often know what's going to happen in the future; in fact, I may have ESP.
The ghost was coming toward us when suddenly it disappeared.
I saw something in the water, but a moment later it was gone.

2. Listen. Check (✓) the transition expressions you hear.

a. ☑ in fact   c. ☐ at the same time   e. ☐ suddenly
   ☐ all of a sudden   ☐ a moment later   ☐ however

b. ☐ but then   d. ☐ and then   f. ☐ a moment later
   ☐ however   ☐ in fact   ☐ but then

C Change partners. Student A is a reporter. Use the questions from Exercise A to interview Student B about the mysterious event. Then change roles.

Could you please tell me what happened?

Well, I looked out my bedroom window, . . .

Listening task 1 • Information

MAIN IDEA **A** 🎧 **Listen. People are talking about the Philippines. What are they talking about? Write the topics in the chart below.**

PHILIPPINES: Fact File

Topics	Information		
1. _____ _____	**Location** _____	**Capital** _____	**Languages** • _Filipino (Tagalog)_ • _____
2. _____	**Nationality** • man: _____ • woman: _____	**Ethnic background** • _____ • _____ • _____	**Character** • _____ • _____ • _____
3. _____	**Agricultural exports** • _____ • _____ • _____ • _____	**Other exports** • _____ • _____ • _____	
4. _____ _____	**Outdoor activities** • _____ • _____ • _____	**Wildlife** • the world's smallest _____ • _____ and _____ in Palawan	

DETAILS **B** 🎧 **Listen again. Complete the missing information in the chart.**

Listening task 2 • Volunteer work

MAIN IDEA **A** Listen. A student is talking about volunteer work in the Philippines. What projects did the student's group do? What were its goals? Complete the missing information.

Projects	Goals
1. *planted trees*	*teach young people about the environment*
2.	
3.	
4.	

DETAILS **B** Listen again. Why did he decide to go on the trip? Number the reasons from 1 to 4. (There is one extra reason.)

_____ to see the Philippines
_____ because of a childhood memory
_____ because of his personality type
__1__ to help protect the environment
_____ because of advice he had received

Appendix | Unit 9 • Trivia game

PREPARE **A** Work with a partner. Student B, use this page. Don't show your page to your classmates! Read the trivia questions and try to guess the missing answers.

Science Trivia Game

What is the longest river on Earth? _____	Are Europe and North America moving closer together or farther apart? *farther apart*	Which is deeper: the Atlantic Ocean or the Pacific Ocean? *the Pacific Ocean*
What is another name for the symbol O_2? *oxygen*	How many times per second does a fly beat its wings? _____	TRUE or FALSE? Frogs breathe through their skin. *true*
TRUE or FALSE? Many years ago, some people thought the earth was flat. *true*	Where is the oldest mountain range on Earth?	How many planets are there in the earth's solar system?

PRACTICE **B** 1. 🎧 Listen and practice. Notice the different pronunciations of *th*.

th = /θ/	th = /ð/
thirty	their
something	farther
Earth	breathe
_____	*another*
_____	_____
_____	_____

2. 🎧 Write the words in the correct columns. Then listen and check your answers.

✓another   breath   northern   south   thought   together

SPEAK **C** Play the game in Exercise A with the class. Go around the room and ask classmates the questions. Write the missing answers on the game board.

Excuse me. What is the longest river on Earth?   *It's the Nile River.*

Answer key

Unit 8 Natural health
Page 36
Warming up
Exercise A

Food and drink
Blueberries can improve memory and eyesight.
Dark chocolate is good for the heart.
Green tea helps prevent cancer.

Natural treatments
Hot springs and mud baths are good for the skin.
Reflexology and massage can relieve problems in certain parts of the body.
Saunas help the body get rid of chemicals.

Herbal medicine
Hot peppers can help the blood circulate.
Garlic helps clean the blood.
Ginger is good for the stomach.

Unit 9 Science trivia
Page 42
Warming up
Exercise B

1. Hot	3. seconds	5. woman's	7. Babies
2. Mosquitoes	4. reflects	6. have more heartbeats	8. toothaches

Unit 16 Unsolved mysteries
Page 72
Warming up
Exercise A

Ghosts	Life in outer space	Mysterious creatures	Psychic abilities
haunted house	UFO	Bigfoot	ESP
phantom	alien	Loch Ness monster	mental telepathy

Activation

A speaking and listening game

- Work in groups of four.
- Put a marker on "Start."
- Close your eyes. Touch the "How many spaces?" box with a pencil. Move that many spaces.
- Follow the instructions.
- Take turns.

Tell about an ad you hate. Why don't you like it?

What topics do you usually talk about when you meet someone?

ANY PLAYER CAN ASK YOU ONE QUESTION.

If you could have a date with a famous person, who would it be? Why?

Imagine you are going to study abroad. Talk about your ideal situation.

Start

What do you do for good luck before an English test?

What do you do to stay healthy? What else should you do?

Finish

Do you do anything to bring good luck? to avoid bad luck?

What's your favorite Web site? Why do you like it?

What are three things that are important to you in a company you work for?

Talk about a communication difference between your culture and another culture you know.

What do people do that you think is very rude? What would you say to them?

Tell about a time you saw something surprising or mysterious.

What was a very difficult decision you had to make?

Say three words that describe the way something tastes.

What do people in your culture do and say when they meet someone for the first time?

Talk about the northern lights. What do you know about them?

Tell about an unusual health treatment you've tried. If you haven't tried one, what would you like to try?

Ask the group a science trivia question. The player who guesses correctly moves ahead one space.

What's a custom in your culture that is hard for foreigners to understand? How could you explain it?

Think of a type of food. Don't tell your classmates! Describe the food. How does it feel? look? smell? taste? Can the other players guess the food?

What do you use the Internet for? Name as many things as you can.

Think of an electronic device. Don't tell your classmates. Describe how the device works. Can the other players guess the device?

YOU CAN ASK ANY PLAYER A QUESTION.

Describe the personality traits of someone you admire.

Tell about an ad you think is really good. Why do you think so?

Imagine you are a company president. What are three things you would do to make the company successful?

What is the best advice you have ever received? Who gave you the advice? When?

ANY PLAYER CAN ASK YOU ONE QUESTION.

How many spaces?					
2	1	3	1	3	2
1	3	4	2	3	1
3	1	2	1	2	3
1	2	1	3	5	2
3	5	2	1	2	3
2	1	3	4	3	1

Name three things that are important to you in a person you date.

If you could change something about your personality, what would it be?

What's a superstition that many people believe? Do you?

What are two things you think are very important to society? Why are they important?

Your neighbors are very noisy every night. You can't sleep. What do you do?

What would make your area a better place to live?

Give advice about studying abroad in your country. Recommend the best location, length of stay, type of school, housing, and any other useful information.

Listening tips

Here are some listening tips to help you become an active listener.

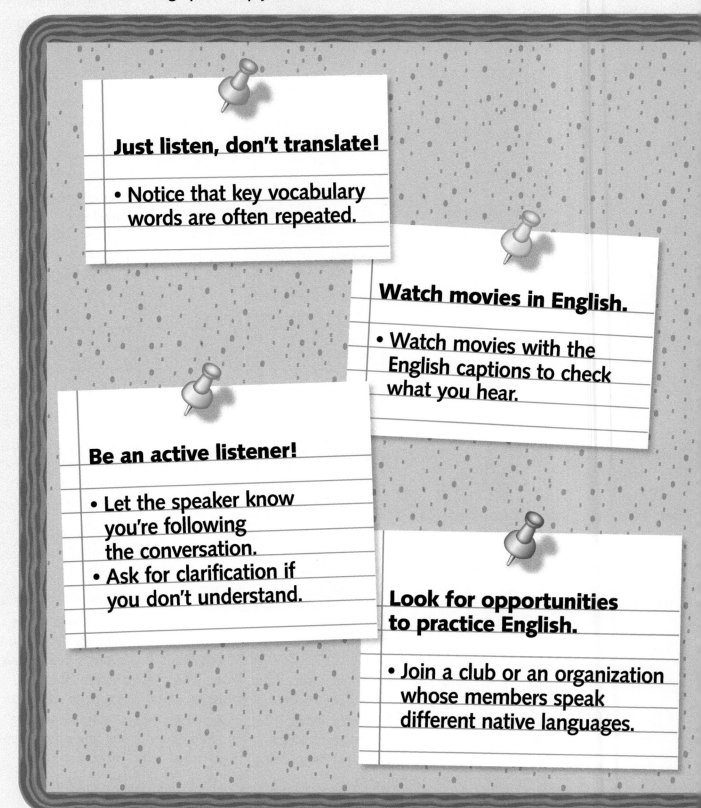

Just listen, don't translate!

- Notice that key vocabulary words are often repeated.

Watch movies in English.

- Watch movies with the English captions to check what you hear.

Be an active listener!

- Let the speaker know you're following the conversation.
- Ask for clarification if you don't understand.

Look for opportunities to practice English.

- Join a club or an organization whose members speak different native languages.

Listen to radio or news programs in English.

- Try to predict the vocabulary you will hear.
- Write the words down before you listen.

Call places with answering machines in English.

- Try to predict the information you will hear.
- Write words or phrases you might hear.
- Circle your predictions as you listen.

Get audio recordings of English books.

- Listen when you can relax and enjoy the story.

Find podcasts for language learners on the Internet.

- Listen to English in a variety of situations.

Self-study

Unit 1

A 1. 🎧 **Listen to the conversation.**

2. 🎧 **Listen again. Circle the correct answers.**

1. The people are
   a. co-workers.
   b. students.
   c. friends.

2. The woman used to work
   a. in Chicago.
   b. near Chicago.
   c. far from Chicago.

3. The man
   a. knows a little about Chicago.
   b. is going to visit Chicago.
   c. is from Chicago.

4. The man is interested in
   a. museums.
   b. concerts.
   c. museums and concerts.

5. The woman is interested in
   a. museums.
   b. concerts.
   c. museums and concerts.

B 🎧 **Listen. Check (✓) *yes* or *no*. Then write your answers.**

yes no
1. ☐ ☐ _____
2. ☐ ☐ _____
3. ☐ ☐ _____
4. ☐ ☐ _____
5. ☐ ☐ _____

Unit 2

A 1. 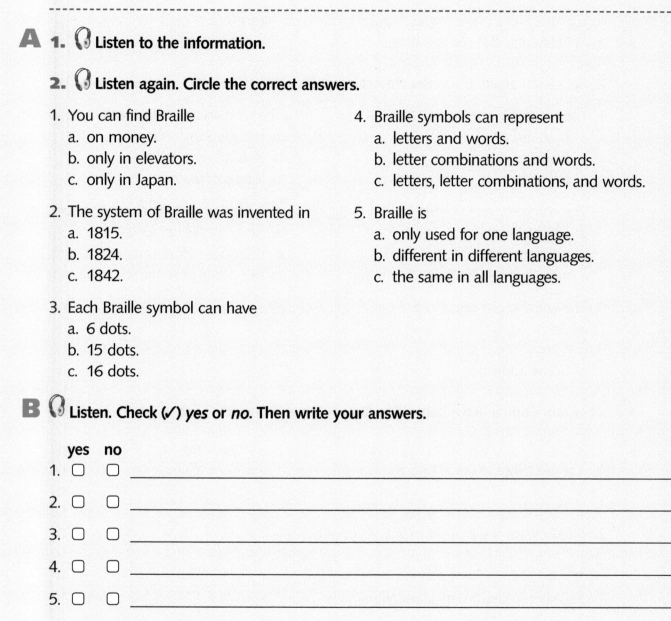 Listen to the information.

2. Listen again. Circle the correct answers.

1. You can find Braille
   a. on money.
   b. only in elevators.
   c. only in Japan.

2. The system of Braille was invented in
   a. 1815.
   b. 1824.
   c. 1842.

3. Each Braille symbol can have
   a. 6 dots.
   b. 15 dots.
   c. 16 dots.

4. Braille symbols can represent
   a. letters and words.
   b. letter combinations and words.
   c. letters, letter combinations, and words.

5. Braille is
   a. only used for one language.
   b. different in different languages.
   c. the same in all languages.

B Listen. Check (✓) *yes* or *no*. Then write your answers.

	yes	no	
1.	☐	☐	_____
2.	☐	☐	_____
3.	☐	☐	_____
4.	☐	☐	_____
5.	☐	☐	_____

Unit 3

A 1. 🎧 **Listen to the conversation.**

2. 🎧 **Listen again. Circle the correct answers.**

1. The woman wants to find a
   a. husband.
   b. friend.
   c. boyfriend.

2. The company requires her to
   a. join with a friend.
   b. pay some money.
   c. write a long description of herself.

3. The woman has to give her
   a. age.
   b. salary.
   c. home address.

4. The woman wants to meet someone who
   a. has the same interests.
   b. doesn't live nearby.
   c. likes computers.

5. The woman can get her money back if
   a. no one asks her for a date.
   b. she doesn't find someone to date.
   c. she doesn't like the man she meets.

B 🎧 **Listen. Complete the sentences. Do you agree? Check (✓) yes or no.**

	yes	no
1. The best way to fall in love is _____ .	☐	☐
2. I really want my partner to get along with _____ .	☐	☐
3. You should never date someone who is _____ .	☐	☐
4. I'd like to meet someone who has _____ .	☐	☐
5. It's important for my partner to have the same _____ .	☐	☐

Unit 4

A 1. 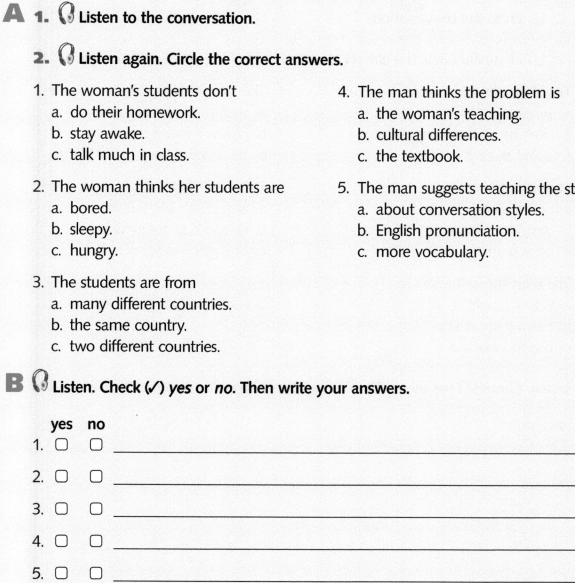 **Listen to the conversation.**

   2. **Listen again. Circle the correct answers.**

   1. The woman's students don't
      a. do their homework.
      b. stay awake.
      c. talk much in class.

   2. The woman thinks her students are
      a. bored.
      b. sleepy.
      c. hungry.

   3. The students are from
      a. many different countries.
      b. the same country.
      c. two different countries.

   4. The man thinks the problem is
      a. the woman's teaching.
      b. cultural differences.
      c. the textbook.

   5. The man suggests teaching the students
      a. about conversation styles.
      b. English pronunciation.
      c. more vocabulary.

B **Listen. Check (✓) *yes* or *no*. Then write your answers.**

	yes	no	
1.	☐	☐	_____
2.	☐	☐	_____
3.	☐	☐	_____
4.	☐	☐	_____
5.	☐	☐	_____

Unit 5

A 1. ◯ **Listen to the conversation.**

2. ◯ **Listen again. Circle the correct answers.**

1. The Web site is for
   a. shopping.
   b. chatting and meeting people.
   c. doing research.

2. The woman
   a. writes a blog.
   b. designs Web sites.
   c. downloads music.

3. The man thinks the site
   a. is too expensive.
   b. has a good design.
   c. has too many ads.

4. The woman likes the site because
   a. she's met a lot of friends.
   b. her best friend uses it.
   c. she doesn't have many friends.

5. The man
   a. is going to join the site.
   b. isn't sure about joining.
   c. isn't going to join.

B ◯ **Listen. Check (✓) yes or no. Then write your answers.**

	yes	no	
1.	☐	☐	_____
2.	☐	☐	_____
3.	☐	☐	_____
4.	☐	☐	_____
5.	☐	☐	_____

Unit 6

A 1. 🎧 **Listen to the conversation.**

2. 🎧 **Listen again. Circle the correct answers.**

1. This weekend, the woman is going to
   a. attend a friend's wedding.
   b. get married.
   c. buy a wedding dress.

2. The superstition is about
   a. living a long time.
   b. finding someone to marry.
   c. having a happy marriage.

3. The woman's wedding dress is
   a. old.
   b. new.
   c. blue

4. The woman needs something
   a. borrowed.
   b. old.
   c. blue.

5. The man will lend the woman
   a. his shoes.
   b. his wedding ring.
   c. a coin.

B 🎧 **Listen. Then check (✓) your answers.**

	It's lucky.	It's unlucky.	It has no special meaning.
1.	☐	☐	☐
2.	☐	☐	☐
3.	☐	☐	☐
4.	☐	☐	☐
5.	☐	☐	☐

Unit 7

A **1.** 🎧 **Listen to the conversation.**

2. 🎧 **Listen again. Circle the correct answers.**

1. The woman has
   a. never used her phone.
   b. used her phone many times.
   c. used her phone once.

2. The people are
   a. at a restaurant.
   b. on the train.
   c. outside.

3. The man thinks using a cell phone in a restaurant is
   a. OK.
   b. strange.
   c. rude.

4. The man says people should not use cell phones
   a. outside.
   b. in class.
   c. around other people's homes.

5. The man
   a. doesn't have a cell phone.
   b. has a cell phone but doesn't use it.
   c. wants to buy a cell phone.

B 🎧 **Listen. Complete the sentences. Do you think the behaviors are rude? Check (✓) yes or no.**

	yes	no
1. A friend meets you for lunch _____ minutes late.	☐	☐
2. A friend sends a _____ for your birthday instead of a _____ .	☐	☐
3. You hear someone talking on a cell phone in the _____ .	☐	☐
4. A neighbor plays loud music until _____ P.M.	☐	☐
5. A person walking in front of you doesn't _____ the _____ .	☐	☐

Unit 8

A 1. 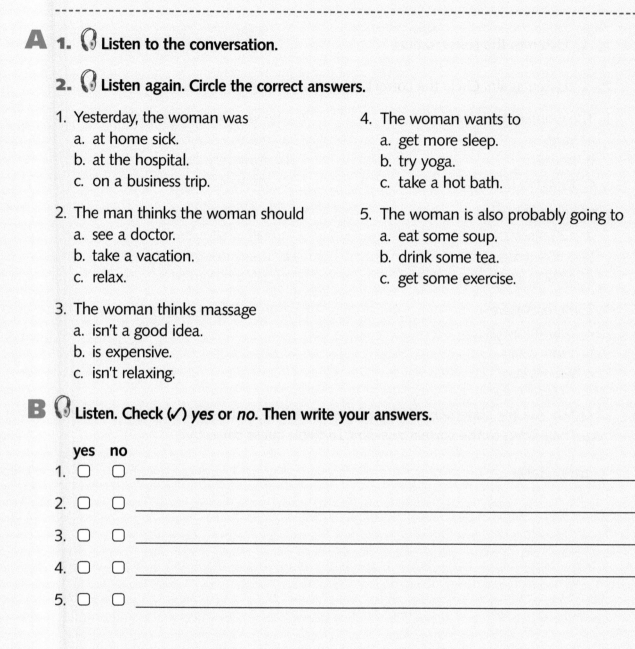 Listen to the conversation.

2. Listen again. Circle the correct answers.

1. Yesterday, the woman was
   a. at home sick.
   b. at the hospital.
   c. on a business trip.

2. The man thinks the woman should
   a. see a doctor.
   b. take a vacation.
   c. relax.

3. The woman thinks massage
   a. isn't a good idea.
   b. is expensive.
   c. isn't relaxing.

4. The woman wants to
   a. get more sleep.
   b. try yoga.
   c. take a hot bath.

5. The woman is also probably going to
   a. eat some soup.
   b. drink some tea.
   c. get some exercise.

B Listen. Check (✓) *yes* or *no*. Then write your answers.

	yes	no	
1.	☐	☐	_____
2.	☐	☐	_____
3.	☐	☐	_____
4.	☐	☐	_____
5.	☐	☐	_____

Unit 9

A **1.** 🎧 Listen to the conversation.

2. 🎧 Listen again. Circle the correct answers.

1. The woman has a bat in her
   a. yard.
   b. house.
   c. garage.

2. In one night, a bat can eat
   a. 120 insects.
   b. 1,200 insects.
   c. 12,000 insects.

3. Some bats have
   a. colorful wings.
   b. short wings.
   c. wide wings.

4. The woman thought bats could
   a. not see at all.
   b. grow very big.
   c. see well.

5. The woman plans to
   a. call a bat expert.
   b. move out of her house.
   c. ask the man to help her.

B 🎧 Listen. Are the statements true or false? Check (✓) your guesses to the science quiz. Then listen to the correct answers. Did you guess correctly?

	true	false
1.	☐	☐
2.	☐	☐
3.	☐	☐
4.	☐	☐
5.	☐	☐

Unit 10

A 1. 🎧 **Listen to the information.**

2. 🎧 **Listen again. Circle the correct answers.**

1. Slogans are used by
   a. most snack food companies.
   b. large corporations.
   c. many types of companies.

2. Slogans are effective because people
   a. remember the brand.
   b. believe the brand is good.
   c. will pay more for the brand.

3. Experts say a slogan should be
   a. serious.
   b. funny.
   c. simple.

4. A good slogan makes people feel
   a. one hundred percent satisfied.
   b. good about the brand.
   c. strong emotions.

5. A telephone company slogan says
   "Reach out and . . ."
   a. touch someone.
   b. call someone.
   c. be someone.

B 🎧 **Listen. Check (✓) *yes* or *no*. Then write your answers.**

	yes	no	
1.	☐	☐	_____
2.	☐	☐	_____
3.	☐	☐	_____
4.	☐	☐	_____
5.	☐	☐	_____

Unit 11

A 1. 🎧 **Listen to the radio advertisement.**

2. 🎧 **Listen again. Circle the correct answers.**

1. The school offers classes in
   a. English.
   b. test preparation.
   c. foreign languages.

2. The class never has more than
   a. four students.
   b. eight students.
   c. eighteen students.

3. The length of the courses is
   a. six days.
   b. six weeks.
   c. six months.

4. The school is located
   a. in several different places.
   b. outside the city.
   c. downtown.

5. The school guarantees
   a. one hundred percent satisfaction.
   b. a discount on future classes.
   c. higher test scores.

B 🎧 **Listen. Check (✓) yes or no. Then write your answers.**

	yes	no	
1.	☐	☐	_____
2.	☐	☐	_____
3.	☐	☐	_____
4.	☐	☐	_____
5.	☐	☐	_____

Unit 12

A 1. 🎧 **Listen to the conversation.**

2. 🎧 **Listen again. Circle the correct answers.**

1. The people are getting ready to
   a. have a dinner party.
   b. go out to dinner.
   c. go shopping.

2. The robot's microprocessor
   a. stores the dirt.
   b. sends signals to the sensors.
   c. tells it what to do.

3. First, the robot
   a. measures the room.
   b. presses the "Clean" button.
   c. waits for the signal.

4. The robot will
   a. turn around.
   b. bump into furniture.
   c. clean the walls.

5. The woman
   a. thinks the device was expensive.
   b. likes the device.
   c. doesn't like the device.

B 🎧 **Listen. Check (✓) yes or no. Then write your answers.**

	yes	no	
1.	☐	☐	_____
2.	☐	☐	_____
3.	☐	☐	_____
4.	☐	☐	_____
5.	☐	☐	_____

Unit 13

A 1. 🎧 **Listen to the conversation.**

2. 🎧 **Listen again. Circle the correct answers.**

1. Brittany's brother was born in
   a. May.
   b. June.
   c. July.

2. Her brother is
   a. confident.
   b. picky.
   c. reserved.

3. Amelia thinks zodiac signs
   a. aren't important.
   b. are important.
   c. don't fit people's personalities.

4. Amelia is
   a. cautious.
   b. extroverted.
   c. emotional.

5. Amelia and Brittany's brother are
   a. a good match.
   b. a little alike.
   c. very different.

B 🎧 **Listen. Write your answers. You need to know these shapes.**
circle = ●   diamond = ◆   square = ■   star = ★   triangle = ▲

Unit 14

A **1.** 🎧 **Listen to the conversation.**

2. 🎧 **Listen again. Circle the correct answers.**

1. The man is worried about his
   a. son's education.
   b. son's graduation.
   c. wife's education.

2. The son wants to
   a. go to college now.
   b. get a full-time job.
   c. go to college later.

3. The man thinks his son
   a. will move abroad.
   b. may never go to college.
   c. won't make enough money.

4. The woman says the son's idea may be
   a. bad for his future.
   b. too dangerous.
   c. a good opportunity.

5. The man will probably
   a. not change his mind.
   b. change his mind.
   c. stop worrying.

B 🎧 **Listen. Check (✓) *very important*, *somewhat important*, or *a little important*.**
Then write your answers to the questions.

	very important	somewhat important	a little important	
1.	☐	☐	☐	_____
2.	☐	☐	☐	_____
3.	☐	☐	☐	_____
4.	☐	☐	☐	_____
5.	☐	☐	☐	_____

Unit 15

A 1. 🎧 **Listen to the conversation.**

2. 🎧 **Listen again. Circle the correct answers.**

1. The man
   a. has changed his job.
   b. wants to change his job.
   c. will change his job soon.

2. The man's new company
   a. makes a lot of garbage.
   b. pays the employees well.
   c. helps the environment.

3. At his last company, the man had
   a. a boring job.
   b. a busy schedule.
   c. an easy schedule.

4. The guiding principle means
   a. employees and customers are important.
   b. customers are the most important.
   c. employees aren't important.

5. The woman wants to
   a. keep her job.
   b. change her job.
   c. open her own company.

B 🎧 **Listen. Write your answers. Then check (✓) yes or no.**

	yes	no
1. _____	☐	☐
2. _____	☐	☐
3. _____	☐	☐
4. _____	☐	☐
5. _____	☐	☐

Unit 16

A 1. 🎧 **Listen to the conversation.**

2. 🎧 **Listen again. Circle the correct answers.**

1. The woman thinks she has
   a. noisy neighbors.
   b. a haunted house.
   c. ESP.

2. First, the man thinks the noise is
   a. the woman's husband.
   b. a ghost.
   c. the woman's child.

3. Next, the man suggests she heard
   a. aliens.
   b. a spirit.
   c. the wind.

4. The woman's husband has
   a. heard the noise.
   b. never heard the noise.
   c. seen a ghost.

5. The man wants to
   a. call the police.
   b. visit the house.
   c. talk to her husband.

B 🎧 **Listen to the story. Imagine the scene. Then listen again. Write the missing words on the lines.**

I had a _____mysterious_____ experience last (summer) .

I was _____ in the (_____) with my (_____) .

Suddenly, I _____ (_____) . Then I saw a

_____ who looked like a (_____) . It _____

a (_____) at me and said, (" _____ . ")

C 🎧 **Listen again. When you hear the bell, write any word in the circle that makes sense. You can choose any word you want.**

Self-study answer key

Unit 1

Exercise A

1. a
2. b
3. a
4. c
5. c

Unit 2

Exercise A

1. a
2. b
3. a
4. c
5. b

Unit 3

Exercise A

1. c
2. b
3. a
4. a
5. b

Exercise B

1. by chance
2. my family
3. much younger
4. a similar personality
5. amount of money as I have

Unit 4

Exercise A

1. c
2. b
3. a
4. b
5. a

Unit 5

Exercise A

1. b
2. a
3. c
4. a
5. c

Unit 6

Exercise A

1. b
2. c
3. b
4. a
5. c

Unit 7

Exercise A

1. a
2. a
3. c
4. b
5. a

Exercise B

1. fifteen
2. card, gift
3. park
4. 9:00
5. hold, door

Unit 8

Exercise A

1. a
2. c
3. b
4. c
5. b

Self-study answer key

Unit 9
Exercise A
1. b
2. b
3. c
4. a
5. c
Exercise B
1. false
2. false
3. true
4. false
5. true

Unit 10
Exercise A
1. c
2. a
3. c
4. b
5. a

Unit 11
Exercise A
1. c
2. b
3. b
4. a
5. a

Unit 12
Exercise A
1. a
2. c
3. a
4. a
5. b

Unit 13
Exercise A
1. a
2. c
3. a
4. b
5. c

Unit 14
Exercise A
1. a
2. c
3. b
4. c
5. a

Unit 15
Exercise A
1. a
2. c
3. b
4. a
5. b

Unit 16
Exercise A
1. b
2. a
3. c
4. a
5. b

Exercise B
I had a **mysterious** experience last (   ).
I was **walking** in the (   ) with my
(   ). Suddenly, I **heard** (   ). Then I saw a
creature who looked like a (   ). It **pointed**
a (   ) at me and said, ("   .")

Self-study track listing

The audio CD contains the Self-study audio exercises from Student's Book 3.

Track	Unit	Page
Track 1	Unit 1	Page 84
Track 2	Unit 2	Page 85
Track 3	Unit 3	Page 86
Track 4	Unit 4	Page 87
Track 5	Unit 5	Page 88
Track 6	Unit 6	Page 89
Track 7	Unit 7	Page 90
Track 8	Unit 8	Page 91
Track 9	Unit 9	Page 92
Track 10	Unit 10	Page 93
Track 11	Unit 11	Page 94
Track 12	Unit 12	Page 95
Track 13	Unit 13	Page 96
Track 14	Unit 14	Page 97
Track 15	Unit 15	Page 98
Track 16	Unit 16	Page 99